Renal Diet Cookbook

1500 days of Wholesome Low Sodium, Phosphorus, & Potassium Recipes to Avoid Dialysis and Reduce Your Kidneys' Disease Symptoms | 4 Weeks Healthy Meal Plan Easy-to-Cook

Gloria Grant

© Copyright 2022 - All rights reserved.

The content contained within this book may not be reproduced, duplicated, or transmitted without direct written permission from the author or the publisher. Under no circumstances will any blame or legal responsibility be held against the publisher, or author, for any damages, reparation, or monetary loss due to the information contained within this book. Either directly or indirectly.

Legal Notice:

This book is copyright protected. This book is only for personal use. You cannot amend, distribute, sell, use, quote, or paraphrase any part, or the content within this book, without the consent of the author or publisher.

Disclaimer Notice:

Please note the information contained within this document is for educational and entertainment purposes only. All effort has been executed to present accurate, up-to-date, reliable, and complete information. No warranties of any kind are declared or implied.

Readers acknowledge that the author is not engaging in the rendering of legal, financial, medical, or professional advice. The content within this book has been derived from various sources, and please consult a licensed professional before attempting any techniques outlined in this book.

By reading this document, the reader agrees that under no circumstances is the author responsible for any direct or indirect losses incurred because of the use of the information contained within this document, including, but not limited to, — errors, omissions, or inaccuracies.

Table of Contents

Table of Contents 3
Introduction 4
The Renal Diet... 5
Benefits Of Renal Diet 9
Recipes 11
Desert Recipes 56
Vegetarian Recipes 72
Index 91
Final Words.. 93

Introduction

This cookbook will show you how to make a tasty, nutritious meal while following a renal diet. This diet is for people who either already have renal failure or are at significant risk of developing it in the future. Rich nutrients are supplemented with protein, vitamins, and minerals from animal diets high in L-carnitines, which may be turned into energy instead of being ejected from the body as waste in the urine.

A nutritionist has reviewed every dish in this cookbook with training, and all ingredients can be found in the low sodium section of your local grocery store. Because renal diets include so many sources of protein, even foods with a high salt content like beef, lamb, and fish can be consumed often.

There is a wealth of knowledge regarding renal diets in this cookbook. Your kidney health affects how much protein you should eat. There is one exception to the rule that most people on a renal diet will need to take protein supplements. Dairy products, eggs, and canned tuna are good protein sources for kidney sufferers since the body quickly metabolizes protein. Complete and incomplete proteins are the two categories into which proteins are divided. Incomplete proteins are found in plants, whereas complete proteins are found in animals, such as chickens or fish. A renal diet includes protein from both sources to ensure the body receives the right amount.

Legumes (beans), cheeses, and peanut butter are a few examples of foods that include plant protein. Since the body may generate these amino acids with the help of carbohydrates and fats, vegetarians should ensure they get enough amino acids (protein) for their bodies. The main sources of carbohydrates in renal diets are whole grains, fruits, and vegetables. If your doctor hasn't told you otherwise, a renal diet consists of all vegetables, including those that are starchy. Starchy veggies include yams, maize, potatoes, and carrots.

It is important to comprehend the daily recommended intake of vitamins and minerals; thus, care should be taken when planning a renal diet. Calcium, magnesium, and iron, as well as vitamins A, B 1, B 2, B 6, C, and E, can be found in several dietary categories. Since spices include anti-oxidants that help prevent illness, they are good for your health. Beta-carotene (vitamin A), lycopene (a carotenoid that gives tomatoes their red color), and lutein, present in leafy green vegetables like spinach or collard greens, are examples of antioxidants found in plants.

According to the Institute of Medicine, adults in the United States should consume 400 IU of vitamin D daily and 2000 mg of calcium. Soybeans, broccoli, milk, cheese, yogurt, and other foods are excellent providers of calcium. Vitamin A is abundant in dairy products, but you should also consume it from foods like carrots and sweet potatoes. The primary protein sources in renal diets include milk, meat (beef, chicken, and turkey), beans, eggs, fish (salmon or cod), peanuts, and soybeans. Based on weight, a renal diet should contain 0.60 g/lb to 1.0 g/lb of protein per day, depending on age. The sources of protein are not limited to meat and vegetables; the amount of protein you eat depends on how well your kidneys work. On a renal diet, worrying about getting enough vitamins and minerals is unnecessary because the dietary fiber in food is the greatest way to get them.

Since salt is high in sodium, a renal diet contains little salt. Other sodium salts, such as kosher salt rather than regular salt, sodium citrate, and sodium alginate, can replace sodium (salt) (from seaweed). However, a renal diet does not allow for the exclusion of all kinds of salt from the diet. Some ingredients, like cheese, have salt in them. But draining the water from frozen vegetables can help reduce the amount of salt in some dishes. The excessive salt content of canned goods can be avoided by substituting fresh ingredients. Fresh food is preferred because you can control the salt content.

The Renal Diet

The kidneys lose their ability to excrete or remove material effectively as renal function diminishes. The patient's electrolyte levels will suffer if the surplus is allowed to remain in the blood. By following a kidney diet, it is even possible to help improve kidney function and stop the course of total renal disease.

Any treatment regimen for a chronic kidney ailment must include a healthy renal diet. A renal diet is low in salt, phosphorus, and protein. Eating high-quality protein and usually limiting fluid intake are frequently emphasized on a renal diet. Some people may need to restrict their potassium and calcium intake. Each patient must collaborate with a renal dietician to create a diet customized to their needs because every person's physiology is different. You should consume healthy kidney foods if you have severe renal failure.

Monitoring your diet and drinking habits could inspire you to lead a healthier lifestyle. Your health is impacted by what you consume, and it will support your efforts to manage your blood pressure, maintain a healthy weight, and down a healthy diet low in fat and salt. Diabetes requires careful food and beverage selection to handle blood pressure. By regulating blood pressure and diabetes, a renal diet can aid in preventing the progression of kidney disease.

The degree of renal failure will determine how strict the diet must be. You can have few to no dietary limitations in the early stages of renal disease. Your doctor could suggest that you reduce your intake if your kidney condition worsens:

- Sodium
- Potassium
- Phosphorus
- Protein
- Fluids.

Consume Foods with Less Sodium & Salt

The salt content typically decreases when "No Added Salt" is mentioned. This is crucial because consuming too much salt can result in blood pressure that is improperly managed and increased thirst, both of which can make it challenging to adhere to your diet's fluid restrictions.

To reduce your sodium intake, you should not consume

- Table salt or any seasoning that contains salt • Salt replacements because they might contain potassium
- Salty meats such as canned ham, bacon, hot dogs, sausage, and bologna.
- Salty snacks like cheese curls, chips, salted walnuts, and salted crackers
- Thoroughly wash any canned fish, vegetables, meats, and legumes.
- Steer clear of freezer dinners, canned soups, and fast noodles.
- Regularly consume fresh meals.

Consume The Right Types of Proteins

Protein is necessary for the development and upkeep of body tissue, and protein also contributes to the body's energy creation and infection prevention. Each day, you should aim for 7-8 ounces of protein. Protein is abundant in meat, including hog, turkey, beef, and chicken.

Fish, seafood, and eggs Three ounces of protein, or about the size of a deck of cards, are equal to one egg, which is one ounce of protein. Eat meals with less protein if you're on a renal diet.

A cooked dish of beef, chicken, or fish weighs roughly 2-3 ounces or the equivalent of a deck of cards. One serving of dairy equals one slice of cheese, half a cup of yogurt, or one cup of milk.

Foods with plant-based proteins:

- Grains
- Nuts
- Beans

The cooked beans' portion is about half a cup. A portion of cooked noodles or cooked rice is a half-cup, and a serving of bread is a single slice.

Consume Drinks & Food with Less Phosphorus

Try to eat less high phosphorus foods like:

- Dairy, Meats, fish, and poultry (you can eat one serving)
- Dairy products Milk and cheese (one 4 oz. serving)
- Avoid this food or eat very less of
    - Black Beans, Lima Beans, Red Beans, White Beans, and Black-eyed Peas
    - Unrefined, Dark, whole grains
    - Refrigerated doughs
    - Vegetables and fruits that are Dried
    - Dark-colored sodas
    - Chocolate

If your doctor prescribes it, you may take a phosphate binder. Phosphorus-free meats, seafood, and pasta should be chosen. The daily maximum is 1000mg.

Choose Heart-Healthy Foods

Broil, grill, bake, stir-fry, or roast food instead of deep-frying. Instead of using butter for cooking, use cooking spray or a tiny bit of olive oil. Trim the meat's fat and take the skin off before eating. Read the food labels and cut back on saturated and trans fats. Low-fat or fat-free milk, yogurt, and cheese are all OK.

Consume Food with Less Amount of Potassium

In severe circumstances, high potassium levels might halt the heart. They can also lead to irregular cardiac rhythms. People with high potassium levels often show no symptoms. If you have concerns about your potassium level, talk to your doctor.

Up to 2000 mg of potassium can be consumed daily by patients.

Foods That Lower Potassium

Apples, pears, peaches, white pasta, bread, carrots, green beans, and rice milk.

White rice, apple, grape, or cranberry juice cooked wheat, grits, and rice grains.

Limit Intake of Fluids

Your doctor might suggest you reduce your liquid intake, depending on your kidney health and recovery rates. It will be necessary for you to eat fewer fluids. Anything that consumes a lot of water needs to be minimized as well. There is a lot of water in soups and meals that melt, such as ice, ice cream, and gelatin. A lot of water can be found in many fruits and vegetables.

The daily allotment for people with severe renal failure is typically four cups of fluid. Or as prescribed by your physician.

Benefits Of Renal Diet

Whether you have kidney disease or another ailment, switching to a renal diet has various advantages. In particular, if you frequently experience kidney infections or other conditions that render this important organ incapable of functioning, it's a healthy way to eat and live. This calls for making adjustments as soon as possible and paying great attention to your symptoms and any changes you see because they may signal the progression of the illness or a rise in renal function. By keeping an eye out for even tiny changes, you can improve your health and take control of your well-being. Whether you have kidney disease or another ailment, adopting a renal diet has some advantages.

The Main Benefits of the Renal Diet

How Healthy Eating Can Help

The main goal of the renal diet is to support kidney health because doing so will benefit many other aspects of your health. Though reaching this stage can still be avoided with careful evaluation of your meal choices, avoiding the subsequent phases is the major goal. The diet gives you control over your health and advancement aside from medical treatment. It can mean the difference between having complete renal failure and a manageable chronic illness that allows you to continue living a normal, happy life despite having kidney problems.

A Drug-Free and Natural Way to Support Your Kidneys is to Eat Well

Your diet significantly impacts kidney health, whether or not the medication is a part of your treatment strategy. While restricting other substances that, if ingested in excess, can cause full renal failure if there are already signs of kidney impairment, some herbs and vitamins can improve the therapeutic qualities of meals and provide additional support to your kidneys. Fresh, unprocessed food promotes the health of your kidneys by making it simpler for your body to digest, absorb, and use nutrients. By selecting natural substitutes, you can also reduce or eliminate your intake of processed sugars and sodium, eliminating the need to continually check the quantity of salt or sugar in your diet.

Frozen fruits and vegetables are preferable to fresh ones if you don't have access to fresh produce because they retain all or the majority of their nutrients. Although they could be used as a substitute if there are no other options, canned fruits and vegetables are commonly processed.

Before including canned vegetables in a meal or dish, give them at least two thorough rinses in water to reduce the amount of sodium they contain. Before serving, drain and rinse the fruit from the can to reduce the sugar content. Before placing any box or can in your grocery cart, always verify the contents and only use these substitutes when fresh or frozen options are unavailable.

Even if your health significantly improves as a result of dietary changes and medical advancements and an increase in kidney function is found, do not lower or stop taking the renal medication until directed to do so by a doctor or medical expert. While medicine should be a part of your treatment strategy, nutrition should still play a significant role in your lifestyle. Any substantial or abrupt modifications to your treatment plan risk stopping progress and, ultimately, doing more harm. Think of your renal diet food and meal choices as a part of a bigger picture that includes exercise, any necessary medical treatment, and leading a healthy lifestyle.

Recipes

Break-Fast Recipes

Holy Eggs

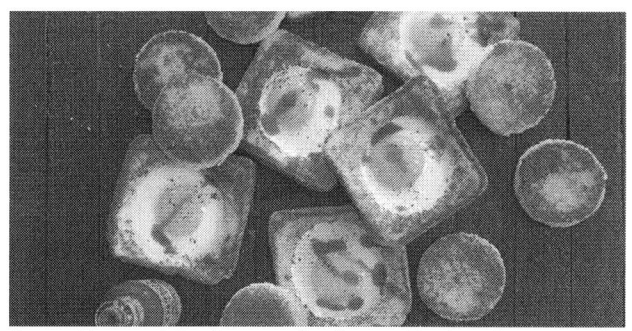

Prep time: 10min, cook time: 5min, Serves: 2

Ingredients

- 4 – eggs, 4 - slices of white bread
- 4 - tsp. margarine,1 – tsp & Tabasco sauce

Direction:

1. Cut a hole in the center of each slice of bread using a small container first.
2. Margarine should then be melted on a nonstick griddle.
3. After that, place bread slices in the container and gently spread margarine over both sides.
4. Cook for 1-2 minutes on a moving object until lightly toasted on one side.
5. the bread cutter over.
6. One egg should be cracked inside the bread cut.
7. Eggs must cook for 2 to 3 minutes before they are done.
8. The bread rounds that were removed and placed with the eggs should be toasted..

Nutrition Facts: calories 359, potassium 93mg, sodium 70mg, phosphorus 12mg, protein 18g.

Lemon Blueberry Surprise Muffins

Prep time: 10min, cook time: 10min, Serves: 9

Ingredients

- 2 teaspoons of baking powder.
- 1/4 cup of heavy cream.
- 1 1/4 cups of vanilla whey protein powder.
- 3 medium eggs, 3 teaspoons of oil.
- Splenda in 5-packs, 1/4-tsp. cinnamo
- 1 teaspoon of lemon rind and 1/2 cup of blueberries
- Cream cheese, 3 ounces, cut into 9 cubes

Direction:

1. Initially, heat the stove to 375°F. Paper liners should be used in 9 biscuit pans.
2. After that, combine the cream, oil, and eggs. Mix together.
3. The whey powder, preparing powder, Splenda, cinnamon, and lemon peel should then be added. until it combines, blend. Avoid over-mixing to avoid tough biscuits.
4. Add the blueberries on top, then carefully scoop half of the mixture into the prepared biscuit pans.
5. Put a 3D cream cheddar square in the center of each.
6. As you add the remaining batter to the tins, make sure to completely cover the cream cheese's 3D designs.
7. Lastly, cook at 375°F for 8–10 minutes, or until the tops are slightly sautéed.

Nutrition Facts: calories 170, potassium 39mg, sodium 162mg, phosphorus 65mg, protein 5g.

New Baked Garlic

Prep time: 25min, cook time: 60min, Serves: 10

Ingredients:

- 1 1/4 cups of vanilla whey protein powder, 1/4 cup of heavy cream, and two teaspoons of baking powder.
- Three medium eggs and three teaspoons of oil
- 5 packs of Splenda, 1/4 teaspoon of cinnamon
- 1/2 cup of blueberries and 1 teaspoon of lemon rind
- 9 cubes of 3 ounces of cream cheese

Direction:

1. Initially, heat the broiler to 375°F.
2. After that, slice garlic bulbs open to reveal cloves.
3. Oil should then be applied, followed by herbs.
4. For 60 minutes, the heat was controlled during treatment.
5. Remove the garlic's skin and enjoy by crushing it!
6. Spread on the toast of your choice

Nutrition Facts: Calories 394g, Fat 21g, Carbs 3.5g, Sugars 1.4g, Protein 22g

Broccoli Dip in French Bread

Prep time: 30min, cook time: 2hrs 10min, Serves: 1

Ingredients:

- 10 oz. of frozen broccoli per package and 1 cup of sour cream
- 1/2 cup low-calorie mayonnaise, 2 tablespoons chopped green onion, including the tips
- 1 tablespoon dried parsley, 1/2 teaspoon dill, and 1 tablespoon garlic powder

Direction:

1. Defrost the broccoli first, then use a paper towel to squeeze out any moisture. Chop broccoli finely. Mayonnaise and harsh cream should be combined well in a small basin.
2. Broccoli and the remaining ingredients are then combined. In any case, refrigerate for two hours. heat the broiler to 350 degrees. French bread's top crust should be cut off, then the inside should be dug out.
3. The removed bread should next be cut into pieces and placed on an ungreased cookie tray. Heat at 350°D e for 8 to 10 minutes, or until gently browned.
4. Spoon into the bread part that has been emptied. dispense with chunks of toasted bread or salt-free wafers..

Nutrition Facts: Calories 208.5g, Fat 9.1g, Carbs 30.5g, Sugars 3g, Protein 12.2g

Deviled Eggs

Prep time: 10min, cook time: 10min, Serves: 4

Ingredients:

- Dash of paprika, Pepper to taste
- 2 - tbsp. mayonnaise, ½ - tsp. dry mustard
- ½ - tsp. vinegar, 1 - tbsp. onion & 4 - hard boiled eggs

Direction:

1. Eggs should first have the yolk removed after being cut lengthwise.
2. Then using a fork, mash the yolks and combine with the remaining ingredients.
3. Eggs are then slightly refilled and piled.
4. Add some paprika.

Nutrition Facts: Calories 145g, Fat 13g, Carbs 0.5g, Sugars 0.5g, Protein 6.5g

New Mexican Nibbles

Prep time: 15min, cook time: 20min, Serves: 6

Ingredients:

- 1 room-temperature egg white and 2 12 teaspoons of chili powder
- 3 cups of Life Cereal, 1/4 teaspoon garlic powder, and 1/2 teaspoon cumin.

Direction:

1. Egg whites are first whipped till foamy. After combining the following 3 ingredients in a bowl, fold them into the egg white. Add the grain and gently combine to coat.
2. After that, spread the mixture onto a treat sheet that has been lightly lubricated.
3. After that, heat for 15 minutes at 325°F while continuously combining. On a sheet, cool.
4. strongly guarded storage.

Nutrition Facts: Calories 125g, Fat 16g, Carbs 2.5g, Sugars 0.2g, Protein 16g

Instant Pot Nuts & Bolts

Prep time: 25min, cook time: 15min, Serves: 20

Ingredients

- 4 cups each of Cheerios and Shreddies cereal.
- 2 cups of cubed white bread, 1/4 cup melted margarine, 1/2 cup oil, and 1/2 tsp. garlic powder
- 1/4 teaspoon black pepper and 1 teaspoon onion powder

Direction:

1. White bread should be placed first and cut into various shapes.
2. After that, combine grains and bread blocks in a huge basin.
3. Next, add softened margarine to a small bowl. Spread margarine on the oat mixture.
4. Blend of oats with oil and seasonings added. Mix well.
5. Spread the mixture onto two cookie sheets. For 60 minutes, heat in a broiler set to 250°F.
6. Cool and keep in a safe container.

Calories 343g, Fat 11g, Carbs 23g, Sugars 2g, Protein 22g

Nectarine Bruschetta

Prep time: 15, minutes difficulty level: low, servings: 2

Ingredients:

- 1.5 tablespoons of white wine vinegar
- Honey, one teaspoon
- One nectarine, sliced
- 1/4 cup of olive oil
- Black pepper, two teaspoons (coarsely crushed)
- fresh ricotta cheese, 1/3 cup
- Bread, two slices

Direction:

1. Honey and white wine vinegar should be thoroughly combined in a cup. Nectarine should be added and marinated for 10 minutes. Add black pepper and drizzle with olive oil.
2. Toast the bread, then spread it with ricotta and top with nectarines and their juices.

Calories: 71kcal | Carbohydrates: 9g | Protein: 2g | Fat: 3g

Egg Muffins With Ham

Total Time: 25 minutes, Difficulty Level: low, Servings: 6

Ingredients:

- deli ham split into nine slices (thin cut)
- a third cup of spinach mince
- Red pepper, sliced and roasted, in a half-cup can
- huge five eggs
- Pesto sauce, one and a half tablespoons
- Feta cheese, crumbled, 1/4 cup
- A little black pepper
  <u>Pinch of salt</u>
  Fresh basil for garnish

Direction:

1. The oven should be preheated to 400 degrees. Using cooking spray on a muffin pan.
2. Be cautious not to let any spaces for the egg mixture to escape into when you cover each muffin pan with 1.5 slices of ham.
3. Roasted red pepper should be placed halfway up the sides of each muffin pan.
4. Add a tablespoon of spinach mince to the top of each red pepper.
5. On top of the pepper and spinach, add a spoonful and a half of feta cheese that has been chopped.
6. Salt, pepper, and eggs are all combined in a bowl. Six muffin tins should receive the mixture evenly divided.
7. Bake the eggs for 15–17 minutes, or until they feel hard and fluffy to the touch.
8. Remove each muffin cup from the tin with care, then top with fresh basil, 1/4 teaspoon pesto sauce, and more roasted red pepper slices.
9. Serve

Nutrition: Calories: 76 ; Carbohydrates: 2.8 · ; Protein: 6.9 · ; Fat: 4.3 · ; Saturated Fat: 1.4

Kale Frittata with Sweet Potato

Total Time: 30 minutes, Difficulty Level: low, Servings: 4

Ingredients:

- Six eggs, big
- One kosher salt grain
- Half-and-half in a cup
- 0.5 teaspoons of pepper (freshly ground)
- Olive oil, two tablespoons
- Sweet potatoes, two cups
- two cups of chopped, tightly packed kale
- two garlic cloves
- A tiny red onion, half
- Goat cheese, three ounces

Direction:

1. The oven should be preheated to 350 degrees. Whisk together eggs, half and half, and pepper.
2. Sweet potatoes should be cooked for 8 to 10 minutes, or until soft and golden, in a 10-inch ovenproof nonstick skillet with one tablespoon heated oil. Remove from the pan and keep warm. Kale, garlic, and onions should be sautéed for 3 to 4 minutes, or until the kale is wilted and soft, before adding the potatoes. Give the vegetables a uniform coating of the egg mixture and cook for an additional 3 minutes. goat cheese is topped with the egg mixture.
3. Bake for 10 to 14 minutes, or until set, at 350°F.

Calories: 285kcal Carbohydrates: 19g Protein: 15g Fat: 14g

Avocado, Black Bean, and Quinoa Salad

Total Time: 30 minutes, Difficulty Level: low, Servings: 4

Ingredients:

- 2.5 cups of quinoa that has been precooked
- Grape tomatoes, one cup
- black beans, one can (10 ounces)
- Olive oil extra virgin, two tablespoons
- sliced avocado, half
- quarter cup lime juice
- a single cup of cilantro leaves
- A quarter teaspoon of lime zest
- Black pepper, ground, to taste
- single garlic clove
- 1/4 teaspoon of salt

Direction:

1. In a bowl, combine two and a half cups of precooked quinoa with one can of rinsed and drained black beans, one cup of grape tomatoes cut in half, and one half of an avocado.
2. In a food processor, combine 1/4 cup lime juice, 1 cup cilantro leaves, 1/2 teaspoon lime zest, 2 tablespoons extra virgin olive oil, 1/4 teaspoon salt, 1 clove of garlic, and 1/2 teaspoon powdered black pepper.
3. Stir in the quinoa mixture, then chill for 15 minutes.

Nutrition: 4g Fat· 2g Protein · 10g Carbs · 3g Fiber

Garlic-Mint Scrambled Eggs

Prep Time: 9 minutes, Cooking Time: 6 minutes, Servings: 2

Ingredients

- Four big eggs
- 14 cup of soy milk
- 1 minced garlic clove
- Chopped fresh mint, 1/4 cup
- according to taste
- Olive oil, 1 tbsp
- freshly grated Parmesan cheese, 1/2 teaspoon

Direction:

1. Eggs, soy milk, and minced garlic are thoroughly incorporated; add mint and pepper to taste.
2. Heat the olive oil in a nonstick skillet over medium heat. Add the egg mixture, stirring continuously while it cooks to the desired doneness.

Nutrition: Calories: 238 Sodium: 192mg Protein:15.2g Potassium: 229mg Phosphorus: 107mg

Healthy Fruit Smoothie

Prep Time: 10 minutes, Cooking Time: 00 minutes, Servings: 2

Ingredients

- 1/3 cup of blueberries, fresh
- 4 large, hulled fresh strawberries and 1/3 cup of raspberries
- 34 cup of water
- almond milk, 1/3 cup
- Honey, two tablespoons

Direction:

1. Blend the blueberries, raspberries, strawberries, milk, honey, and other ingredients in a food processor. Puree under cover until smooth. Pour into serving glasses.

Nutrition: Calories: 284 Sodium: 15mg Protein: 2.6g Calcium: 26mg Potassium: 326mg Phosphorus: 117mg

Zucchini with Egg

Prep Time: 6 minutes, Cooking Time: 14 minutes, Servings: 2

Ingredients:

- Olive oil, 1/2 tablespoon
- Huge slices of two large zucchini
- To taste, black peppercorns
- 2 substantial egg whites

Direction:

1. Olive oil should be heated in a skillet over medium-high heat before the zucchini is sautéed for about 10 minutes, or until soft. Add black pepper according to taste.
2. In a bowl, whisk the egg whites. Pour the eggs over the zucchini. Cook and stir for 5 minutes, or until the eggs are scrambled and no longer runny. Add black pepper to the eggs and zucchini before cooking. Serve right away and delight.

Nutrition: Calories: 99 Total Sodium: 66mg Protein: 7.5g Potassium: 91mg Phosphorus: 71mg

Green Slime Smoothie

Prep Time: 7 minutes, Cooking Time: 00 minutes, Servings: 2

Ingredients:

1 cup kale
1 cup blueberries
1 tablespoon honey
¼ cup ice

Direction:

Combine the kale, blueberries, honey, and ice in a blender. Blend until smooth. Serve immediately.

Nutrition: Calories: 90 Sodium: 15mg Protein: 1.6g Calcium: 46mg Potassium: 226mg Phosphorus: 171mg

Goat Cheese and Spinach Egg Muffs

Total time: 45 minutes, difficulty level: low, servings: 12

Ingredients:

- Olive oil, one tablespoon
- Kosher pepper with salt
- a substantial red pepper
- 1/4 cup fresh goat cheese crumbles
- two scallions, diced
- 0.5 cup of milk
- Six eggs, big
- one 5-ounce package of chopped baby spinach

Direction:

1. Preheat oven to 350 degrees. Coat a 12-cup muffin pan with nonstick spray.
2. Big skillet oil. Red pepper should be tender after 8 minutes. After turning off the heat, add the scallions.
3. In a large bowl, combine the eggs, milk, salt, and pepper. Red pepper and spinach are in another bowl.
4. Bake for 20 to 25 minutes, or until the middle is just set. (Frittata topping may be damp from spinach even after setting.)
5. Five minutes on a wire rack after removing from pan. Asap. Five minutes on a wire rack after removing from pan. Asap. Five minutes on a wire rack after removing from pan. Asap. Five minutes on a wire rack after removing from pan. Asap. After chilling for 4 days, reheat for 30 seconds on high.

Calories: 98kcal | Carbohydrates: 1g | Protein: 7g | Fat: 7g | Saturated Fat: 3g

Fruit and Cheese Breakfast Wrap

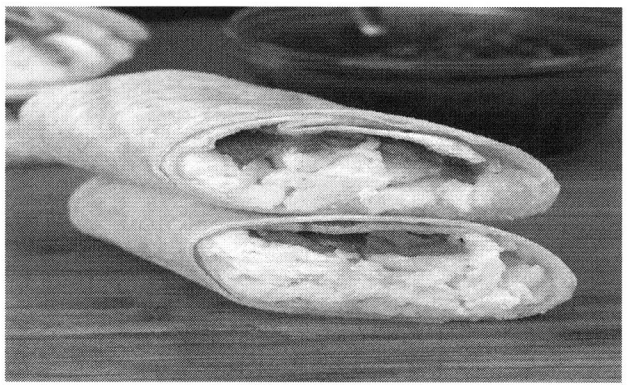

Prep Time: 12 minutes, Cooking Time: 0 minutes, Servings: 2

Ingredients:

- Two flour tortillas (6-inch)
- 2 tbsp. of plain cream cheese
- Apple - 1, cored, peeled, and thinly sliced
- 1 tablespoon honey.

Direction:

1. Spread 1 tablespoon of cream cheese onto each tortilla, leaving approximately 12 inch around the borders, and place both tortillas on a spotless work area.
2. Place the apple slices on top of the cream cheese, leaving about 1 1/2 inches on either side and 2 inches at the bottom. Do this on the tortilla's side that is closest to you.
3. Lightly drizzle some honey over the apples.
4. Laying the edge of the tortilla over the apples, fold the left and right edges toward the center.
5. Fold the edge of the tortilla closest to you over the side pieces and the fruit.
6. The tortilla should be rolled away from you to form a tight wrap.
7. The second tortilla should then be used.

Nutrition: Calories: 188 kcal Total Fat: 6 g Sodium: 177 mg Total Carbs: 33 g Protein: 4 g

Mozzarella Cheese Omelet

Prep time: 8 minutes, Cooking time: 6 minutes, Servings: 1

Ingredients:

- 4 beaten eggs
- 4 tomato slices and 1/4 cup of shredded mozzarella cheese
- A quarter-teaspoon of Italian seasoning
- 1/fourth of a teaspoon dried oregano
- Pepper
- Salt

Direction:

1. Mix eggs and salt in a small bowl.
2. Apply cooking spray to the pan and warm it up over medium heat.
3. Over medium heat, cook the egg mixture in the pan.
4. When the eggs are done, top with oregano and Italian spice.
5. Add shredded cheese and tomato slices to the omelet's surface.
6. For one minute, cook the omelet.
7. Offer and savor.

Nutrition: Calories: 285 Fat: 19g Carbohydrates: 4g Sugar: 3g Protein: 25g Cholesterol: 655mg

Herb Frittata

Total Time: 40 minutes, Difficulty Level: low, Servings: 4

Ingredients:

- /4 cup of crème fraîche Six large eggs and two teaspoons of chopped chives d)
- Olive oil, four tablespoons
- Scallions, six (one inch pieces)
- two cups of leaves of cilantro
- two cups of parsley leaves, flat leaf
- Pepper
- Dill fronds in a half-cup
- Halal salt

Direction:

1. The oven should be preheated to 350 degrees. In a small bowl, combine crème fraiche and chives; place in the refrigerator until required.
2. Slice and finely chop the scallions, cilantro, parsley, dill, and two tablespoons of oil in a food processor. Add to the bowl containing the eggs and stir in the half teaspoon of salt and half teaspoon of pepper.
3. The remaining two teaspoons of oil should shimmer after about two minutes of medium heat in a medium skillet. Add egg mixture and stir until well combined. Cook for about 2 minutes, or until edges start to sear and firm. Bake skillet in oven for 18 to 20 minutes, or until center is barely set. n. Rest for at least five minutes. Add crème fraiche chives as a garnish. If preferred, add more herbs as a garnish.

Calories: 269 calories · Sugar: 1 gram · Fat: 20 grams · Carbohydrates: 2 grams · Fiber: 0 grams · Protein: 19g

Spinach-Curry Crepes

Total Time: 40 minutes, Difficulty Level: low, Servings: 6

Ingredients:

- two enormous eggs
- a third cup of fresh cilantro, chopped coarsely.
- 1/4 teaspoon of black pepper
- 2 1/2 cups of 1% milk
- 2 tablespoons plus 1 cup of all-purpose flour
- Safflower oil, three tablespoon
- 3.4 teaspoons of kosher salt
- one little yellow onion, dice
- Chickpeas in one can, rinsed and drain
- one apple, dice
- 1/4 cup of golden raisins
- Madras curry powder, two tablespoons
- Fresh spinach weighing 10 ounces
- slice of lemon

Direction:

1. Blend eggs, cilantro, pepper, 1 cup flour, 1 cup milk, 2 tablespoons oil, and 1/4 teaspoon salt. Cooking Lightly spray a 10-inch nonstick skillet and heat over medium. Spread 1/3 cup batter on the pan and cook until firm, about 1 minute. 30 seconds. Keep making crepes. Cover to keep warm.
2. Heat the last tablespoon of oil over medium heat. Onion cooks in 5 minutes. Chickpeas, curry powder, apple, and raisins. 3-minutes Cook for 30 seconds while mixing in remaining flour. Include 1.5 cups of milk. 2 minutes. In a larger bowl, combine spinach with remaining salt. About 2 minutes. Fold crepes in half and top with lemon slices..

Nutrition: 327 calories, 13 g protein, 47 g carb, 6 g fiber, 13 g sugars, 11 g fat (2 g sat fat), 541 mg sodium

Beef Recipes

Beef With Mushrooms

Prep Time: 12 minutes | Cook Time: 14 minutes | Serve: 1

Ingredients:

For Beef
- beef tenderloin fillet, trimmed, 4 ounces
- if necessary, salt and freshly ground black pepper 1/4 teaspoon olive oil split
- 14 teaspoon crushed garlic
- 14 teaspoon chopped fresh thyme

For Mushrooms
- a quarter cup of olive oil
- 14 pound of freshly chopped mushrooms and 14 teaspoon of crushed garlic
- if needed, salt and freshly ground black pepper

Direction:
1. For beef, equally season the beef fillet with black pepper and salt before setting it aside.
2. The garlic and thyme are sautéed for approximately a minute in oil that has been heated to medium heat in a cast-iron sauté pan. Cook the fillet for about 5-7 minutes on each side after adding it.
3. In the meantime, prepare the mushrooms by heating the oil in a different cast-iron sauté pan over medium heat and sautéing the mushrooms for 7-8 minutes while tossing constantly.
4. The fillet should be placed on a serving platter. Add the mushroom mixture on top, then plate.
5. Each Serving:

Calories: 291 | Fat: 13.5g | Carbohydrates: 4.1g | Fiber: 1.4g | Sugar: 2g Protein: 35.6g | Sodium: 225mg

Beef With Bell Peppers

Prep Time: 13 minutes | Cook Time: 12 minutes | Serve: 1

Ingredients:
- Olive oil, 1/2 tablespoon
- 14 pound of trimmed and thinly sliced flank steak
- finely sliced, seeded tiny bell pepper
- 14 teaspoon minced fresh ginger
- Low-sodium soy sauce, 1/4 cup
- 1/4 cup balsamic vinegar
- black pepper, ground as needed

Direction:
1. Over medium-high heat in a cast-iron wok, heat the oil and sear the steak pieces for about 2 minutes. While continuously stirring, add the bell peppers and simmer for about 2-3 minutes. The beef mixture should be placed in a bowl using a slotted spoon.
2. Over medium heat, combine the remaining ingredients in the wok and bring to a boil. Stirring constantly, cook for approximately one minute. Add the meat mixture and stir-fry for a few seconds.
3. Serve warm.

Calories: 153 | Fat: 7.3g | Carbohydrates: 2.6g | Fiber: 0.7g | Sugar: 1.3g Protein: 16.6g | Sodium: 165mg

Basil Ground Beef

Prep Time: 11 minutes | Cook Time: 16 minutes | Serve: 1

Ingredients:

- Olive oil, 1/2 tablespoon
- 14 of a chopped onion
- 12 of a minced garlic clove
- 12 teaspoon minced fresh ginger
- 14 lb. of lean ground beef
- 1 teaspoon of basil leaves, fresh
- if needed, salt and freshly ground black pepper

Direction:

1. To cook the onion, heat oil in a small skillet over medium heat for about 5 minutes. With a wooden spoon, break up the ground beef as it cooks for about 8 to 10 minutes with the salt and pepper.
2. After adding the basil, salt, and black pepper, turn off the heat.
3. Serve warm.

Nutrition: Calories: 286 | Fat: 12.5g | Carbohydrates: 3.1g | Fiber: 0.7g | Sugar: 1.2g Protein: 34.9g | Sodium: 231mg

Ground Beef With Cabbage

Prep Time: 10 minutes | Cook Time: 12 minutes | Serve: 1

Ingredients:

- a quarter cup of sesame oil
- 14 lb. of lean ground beef
- 14 teaspoon minced fresh ginger
- 1 minced garlic clove
- 4 ounces of chopped cabbage
- Low-sodium soy sauce, 1 tbsp
- 1/4 cup balsamic vinegar vinegar

Direction:

1. For 5 to 6 minutes, cook the beef, ginger, and garlic in a pan at a medium-high heat. After adding the cabbage, cook for a further 4-5 minutes. Add the vinegar and soy sauce and cook for one minute.
2. Serve warm.

Nutrition: Calories: 273 | Fat: 10.5g | Carbohydrates: 7.1g | Fiber: 2.2g | Sugar: 3.3g Protein: 36.7g | Sodium: 465mg

Beef Avocado Cup

Prep Time: 10 minutes | Serve: 1

Ingredients:

- Pitted half an avocado and a teaspoon of lime juice
  - 14 cup cooked and shredded beef
  - tablespoons of shredded lettuce
  - 2 tablespoons of chopped tomato
- 12 teaspoon finely sliced onion

Direction:

1. From the avocado half, carefully remove about 2 teaspoons of flesh. Chop the avocado flesh, then set it aside.
2. Place the avocado halves on a platter and squeeze little lime juice over each one.
3. The remaining ingredients should be combined thoroughly in a bowl.
4. Serve the meat mixture in the avocado half right away.

Calories: 228 | Fat: 12.5g | Carbohydrates: 6.5g | Fiber: 4.2g | Sugar: 1.2g Protein: 18.6g | Sodium: 42mg

Lemony Pork Chop

Prep Time: 14 minutes | Cook Time: minutes | Serve: 1

Ingredients:

- a quarter cup of olive oil
- 1/four cup Worcestershire sauce
  - 12 teaspoon of lemon juice, fresh
  - 1/8 teaspoon of pasted garlic
  - if needed, salt and freshly ground black pepper
- 1 boneless pork chop, 6 ounces

Direction:

1. In a sizable bowl, combine all the ingredients—aside from the pork chop—and stir thoroughly. Add the pork chop and generously cover with the mixture. For about 15 minutes, cover the bowl and leave it at room temperature.
2. The pork chop should be cooked for about 5 minutes, carefully shaking the pan once or twice during that time. Heat an oiled skillet over medium-high heat. Turn the pork chop over, then lower the heat. For two to three minutes, cook.
3. Serve warm

Calories: 278 | Fat: 9.5g | Carbohydrates: 0.9g | Fiber: 0g | Sugar: 0.8g Protein: 44.6g | Sodium: 275mg

Rosemary Lamb Chop

Prep Time: 12 minutes | Cook Time: 13 minutes | Serve: 1

Ingredients:

- 12 minced garlic clove 14 teaspoon chopped fresh rosemary
  - if needed, salt and freshly ground black pepper
- 1 (6-ounce) chunk of lamb loin

Direction:

1. Heat the grill to a high temperature. Grease the grates on the grill.
2. Garlic, rosemary, salt, and black pepper should all be combined in a basin. Apply a large amount of the herb mixture to the lamb chop.
3. Cook the chop for about two minutes on each side on the hot side of the grill. The chop should now be moved to the cooler side of the grill and cooked for 6-7 minutes.
4. Serve warm.

Calories: 321 | Fat: 12.5g | Carbohydrates: 1g | Fiber: 0.4g | Sugar: 0g Protein: 45.6g | Sodium: 265mg

Lamb Koftas

Prep Time: 12 minutes | Cook Time: 22 minutes | Serve: 1

Ingredients:

- 14 lb. of lean ground lamb
- 12 tablespoon plain, fat-free Greek yogurt
  - 12 tbsp grated onion
  - 12 teaspoon minced garlic
  - 12 teaspoon minced fresh cilantro
  - 1/4 teaspoon of coriander, ground
  - 14 teaspoon of cumin, ground
  - a quarter-teaspoon of ground turmeric
  - if needed, salt and freshly ground black pepper
- Olive oil, 1/2 tablespoon

Direction:

1. All the components should be mixed thoroughly in a bowl. From the ingredients, form 3 equal-sized oblong patties.
2. The patties should be cooked for about 10 minutes, turning them over occasionally, or until they are browned on both sides in a small nonstick skillet.
3. Serve warm.

Calories: 281 | Fat: 14.5g | Carbohydrates: 1.8g | Fiber: 0.3g | Sugar: 0.7g Protein: 32.5g | Sodium: 120mg

Spiced Beef Meatballs

Prep Time: 10 minutes | Cook Time: 20 minutes | Serve: 1

Ingredients:

- 14 lb. of ground beef
- a quarter cup of olive oil
  - 14 teaspoon crumbled dehydrated onion flakes
  - 1/8 teaspoon of garlic granules
  - a pinch of cumin powder
  - Crushed red pepper flakes in a pinch
- Add salt as needed.

Direction:

1. Turn on the oven to 400 °F. Put parchment paper on a little baking sheet.
2. Place all the ingredients in a mixing bowl and, using your hands, stir everything together thoroughly. Create balls of the desired size and shape out of the mixture.
3. Place the meatballs on the baking sheet that has been prepared in a single layer, and bake for 15 to 20 minutes, or until done.
4. Serve warm.

Calories: 245 | Fat: 10.5g | Carbohydrates: 0.9g | Fiber: 0.2g | Sugar: 0.3g Protein: 32.6g | Sodium: 230mg

Beef Avocado Cup

Prep Time: 10 minutes | Serve: 1

Ingredients:

- Pitted half an avocado and a teaspoon of lime juice
  - 14 cup cooked and shredded beef
  - tablespoons of shredded lettuce
  - 2 tablespoons of chopped tomato
- 12 teaspoon finely sliced onion

Direction:

1. From the avocado half, carefully remove about 2 teaspoons of flesh. Chop the avocado flesh, then set it aside.
2. Place the avocado halves on a platter and squeeze little lime juice over each one.
3. The remaining ingredients should be combined thoroughly in a bowl.
4. Serve the meat mixture in the avocado half right away.

Calories: 228 | Fat: 12.5g | Carbohydrates: 6.5g | Fiber: 4.2g | Sugar: 1.2g Protein: 18.6g | Sodium: 42mg

Roast Beef

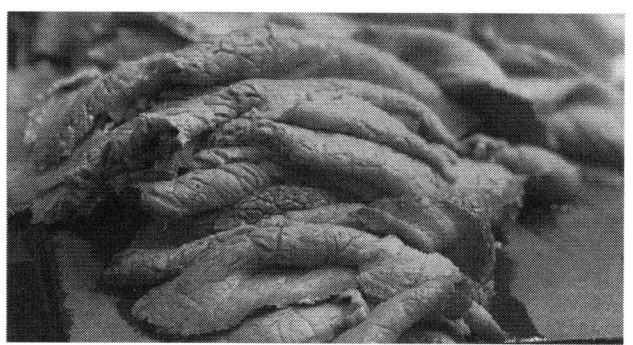

Prep Time: 25 minutes Cooking Time: 55 minutes Servings: 3

Ingredients:

- Quality rump or sirloin tip roast
- Pepper & herbs

Direction:

1. Place on a shallow rack in a roasting pan. Add pepper and herbs for seasoning. Place a meat thermometer in the roast's thickest area or center.
2. Roast until the food is the ideal doneness. Allow it to cool after removing it from the oven for about 15 minutes. The roast should ultimately be moister than well-done.

Nutrition: Calories 158 Protein 24 g Fat 6 g Carbs 0 g Phosphorus 206 mg Potassium 328 mg Sodium 55 mg

Spiced Lamb Burgers

Prep Time: 10 minutes Cooking Time: 20 minutes Servings: 2

Ingredients:

- Extra virgin olive oil, 1 tablespoon
    - 1/2 a red onion, coarsely chopped, and 1 teaspoon cumin
    - 1 minced clove of garlic
    - 1 teaspoon of harissa seasoning
    - Arugula, 1 cup
    - Juiced lemon, one
    - Lean 6-ounce ground lamb
    - a teaspoon of parsley
- 12 cup plain, low-fat yogurt

Direction:

1. Set the broiler to a medium-high heat setting. Olive oil, ground lamb, red onion, parsley, and Harissa spices should all be blended thoroughly.
2. Using wet hands, form patties that are 1 inch thick. Place the patties on a baking sheet and broil for 7 to 8 minutes on each side. With the side salad of arugula, top the lamb patties with a yogurt, lemon juice, and cumin mixture.

Nutrition: Calories 306 Fat 20g Carbs 10g Phosphorus 269mg Potassium 492mg Sodium 86mg Protein 23g

Pork Loins with Leeks

Prep Time: 10 minutes Cooking Time: 35 minutes Servings: 2

Ingredients:

- Sliced leek, one
- 1/4 cup mustard seeds
- 6 oz. pork tenderloin
- 10 grams of cumin seed
- 1/9 cup dried mustard
- 1 tablespoon of virgin olive oil

Direction:

1. The broiler should be preheated to medium-high heat. Heat the mustard and cumin seeds in a dry skillet until they begin to pop (3-5 minutes). Using a mortar and pestle or a blender, grind the seeds, and then include the dried mustard.
2. Pork should be rubbed with the mustard mixture on all sides before being placed on a baking sheet and broiling for 25 to 30 minutes, or until well cooked. halfway through, turn.
3. Remove and set aside, then add the leeks to a pan with the oil and cook for 5–6 minutes, or until tender. Enjoy the pork tenderloin after placing it on a bed of leeks!

Nutrition: Calories 139 Fat 5g Carbs 2g Phosphorus 278mg Potassium 45mg Sodium 47mg Protein 18g

Bacon-Wrapped Mozzarella Sticks

Prep time: 10 minutes Cook time: 3 minutes Serves: 2

Ingredients:

- 1 refrigerator cheese heads a stick of mozzarella cheese
- 2 bacon pieces
- frying using coconut oil
- Pizza sauce with less sugar for dipping
- Toothpicks

Direction:

1. In a deep fryer, heat the coconut oil to 350 degrees.
2. Put the bacon around your thickly sliced cheddar sticks, covering a little bit each step to keep the bacon in place. Apply a toothpick toward the end of the wrapping to hold it in place. Really, it works out better that way to not cover the bargains' components with bacon.
3. Drop the bacon-wrapped cheddar into the hot oil, and cook for two to three minutes, or until the bacon is crisp and extremely black in color.
4. Move away to a paper towel to cool for a few seconds. Take out the toothpick and enjoy with your favorite dipping sauce.

Nutrition: Calories 148, Fat 11g, Carbs 13g, Protein 2g

Poultry Recipes

Crispy chicken wraps

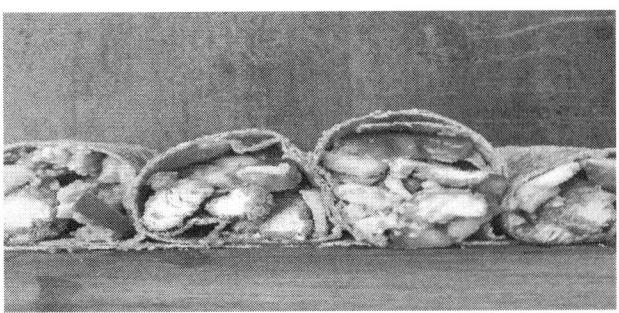

Prep time: 15 min cooking time: 15 min
Servings: 4

Ingredients:

- 1 celery stick, 1/2 red pepper
  - 1 large carrot
  - 60 grams of low-fat mayo
  - 4 whole grain tortillas or 2 whole grain lavash
  - 1/2 tsp of onion powder
- 225 g of chicken in cans (low sodium)

Direction:

1. Cut up bell peppers, celery, and carrots. In a small mixing bowl, combine mayonnaise and onion powder.
2. Each lavash flatbread should receive 2 tbsp of the mixture, and each tortilla should receive 1 tbsp of the mixture.
3. Put the chopped vegetables in another bowl.
4. Place 120g of chicken and half of the vegetables on one side of each flatbread. If using, place 55g of chicken and 1/4 of the vegetables on each tortilla half.
5. To cut each flatbread in half diagonally, roll it up first. Each side is held together by a toothpick. If you're substituting tortillas for lavash, fasten each tortilla with a toothpick before cutting it in half and serving.

Nutrition: Protein: 17 g , Fat: 9 g, Net Carbohydrates: 27 g

Italian Chicken Salad

Prep Time: 5 cooking time: 0 min Servings: 4

Ingredients:

- 115 grams of mayo
- One cayenne peppercorn
  - Lemon juice, 60 ml
  - 4 cooked chicken breasts
  - a sweet onion, 15 g
  - 6 Italian parsley sprigs
  - 1 pepper, yellow or red
  - 250g of zucchini
- Arugula, 40 g

Direction:

1. Two parsley sprigs should be cut into small pieces. Slice the bell pepper and onion finely. Make crescent-shaped zucchini slices.
2. Combine lemon juice, mayonnaise, cayenne pepper, and chopped parsley in a mixing dish (optional). Cut the chicken into 1.5 cm chunks.
3. Toss the chopped onion, chicken, peppers, and zucchini with the mayonnaise to coat.
4. To allow the flavors to meld, chill the dish for at least an hour.
5. Serve with half of the romaine lettuce or arugula. Finish by adding the remaining parsley as a garnish.

Nutrition: Protein: 30 g , Fat: 29 g, Net Carbohydrates: 10 g

Apple Chicken Crispy Salad

Prep time: 10 cooking time: 5 min Servings: 4

Ingredients:

- Apple Gala, 120 g
  - 110 g cooked celery and 280 g chicken
  - 40 g raisins, dark
  - a cup of spring onions
  - 1 teaspoon lemon juice
  - 75 grams of low-fat mayo
  - 1 tablespoon of sour cream (low-fat)
  - One little cinnamon stick
- a little pepper

Direction:

1. Cook the chicken after cubing it. Juice the apple and celery. Chop the spring onions finely.
2. Combine the apple, chicken, celery, raisins, and green onions in a large salad bowl.
3. Mayonnaise, lemon juice, sour cream, black pepper, and cinnamon should all be combined in a mixing dish. Chicken and apples together with the sauce.
4. Until you're ready to serve, keep in the refrigerator.

Nutrition: Protein : 21 g, Fat: 12 g, Net Carbohydrates: 13g

Chicken Scampi

Prep Time: 10 minutes Cooking Time: 20 minutes Servings: 4

Ingredients:

- 14 cup olive oil and 1/2 cup butter
- 1 teaspoon each of dried parsley and basil
  - 1/4 teaspoon dried oregano
  - 3 minced garlic cloves, 1/4 teaspoon salt
  - Lemon juice, 1 tablespoon
- 4 boneless, skinless chicken breast halves, divided into thirds lengthwise

Direction:

1. Chop the red peppers and green onions.
2. Trim the Brussels sprouts' ends, then boil or steam them until they are barely soft.
3. Cook pasta as directed on the package, but without adding salt.
4. Brussels sprouts should be drained and left aside while pasta is cooking.
5. Green onions are sauteed in hot butter and oil in a skillet.
6. Stir in the Brussels sprouts and red peppers, finishing with a slight browned edge.
7. When the macaroni is ready, stir in the soy sauce and cover the vegetable mixture.
8. If necessary, microwave chicken to rewarm it.
9. Combine cooked vegetables, chicken, and macaroni in a bowl.
10. Serve when still heated.

Nutrition: Calories: 402; Total Fat: 27.6g; Saturated Fat: 12g; Cholesterol: 138mg; Sodium: 480mg.

Chicken and Apple Curry

Prep Time: 10 minutes Cooking Time: 1 hour and 11 minutes Servings: 8

Ingredients:
- 8 chicken breasts, boneless and skinless
- Black pepper, 1/4 teaspoon
    - sliced, cored, and peeled two medium apples
    - 2 sliced tiny onions
    - 1 minced garlic clove
    - 3 tbsp. butter
    - Curry powder, 1 tablespoon
    - 0.5 tablespoons dried basil
    - 3 tablespoons of flour
    - Chicken broth, one cup
- 1 cup almond rice milk

Direction:

1. Set the oven to 350°F.
2. Place the chicken breasts in a baking dish and season with black pepper.
3. Melt the butter in a suitable-sized pot over medium heat.
4. Sauté the apple, onion, and garlic until tender.
5. After adding the basil and curry powder, simmer for one minute.
6. Add the flour and mix for a further minute.
7. Add the chicken stock, rice, and almond milk, and stir. Cook for 5 minutes.
8. Over the chicken breasts in the baking pan, pour this sauce.
9. Serve the chicken after baking it for 60 minutes.

Nutrition: Calories: 232 kcal; Total Fat: 8g; Saturated Fat: 0g; Cholesterol: 85mg.

Turkey & Veggie Salad

Prep Time: 10 minutes | Serve: 1

Ingredients:

- 1/4 pound cooked turkey meat, chopped; 1/4 cup green cabbage, shredded; and 1/4 of an English cucumber, chopped
- 1 teaspoon chopped fresh mint leaves
- a quarter cup of olive oil
- 1/4 cup fresh lime juice
- if needed, salt and freshly ground black pepper

Direction:

1. In a salad bowl, add all ingredients and toss to coat well.
2. Serve immediately.

Calories: 240 | Fat: 9.3g | Carbohydrates: 4g | Fiber: 1g | Sugar: 1.8g Protein: 34g | Sodium: 240mg

Turkey Lettuce Wraps

Prep Time: 10 minutes | Cook Time: 20 minutes | Serve: 1

Ingredients:

- 3 ounces of lean ground turkey, 1/4 cup minced onion, and 1/2 cup olive oil
- 14 cup chopped fresh mushrooms
- an eighth of a teaspoon of cayenne
- 1/8 teaspoon of cumin, ground
- two substantial romaine lettuce leaves
- 14 teaspoon chopped fresh cilantro leaves

Direction:

1. Over medium heat, add oil to a skillet and sauté onion for about 4-5 minutes. Cook for 6 to 8 minutes with the turkey, stirring periodically.
2. Cook for about 5-7 minutes after adding the mushrooms, ginger, tamari, cayenne pepper, and cumin. Heat has been removed; set aside.
3. The lettuce leaves should be arranged on serving plates. Evenly distribute the turkey mixture over each lettuce leaf.
4. Serve, then sprinkle equally with cilantro..

Calories: 196 | Fat: 13.3g | Carbohydrates: 3g | Fiber: 0.8g | Sugar: 1.3g Protein: 17.6g | Sodium: 70mg

Seasoned Turkey Legs

Prep Time: 10 minutes | Cook Time: 1 hour and 40 minutes | Serve: 1

Ingredients:

- 1 skinless, boneless turkey leg
- Olive oil, 1/2 tablespoon
  - 1/4 tsp. dry thyme
  - 1/4 teaspoon seasoning for poultry
  - if needed, salt and freshly ground black pepper
- 14 cup of chicken broth low in salt

Direction:

1. Turn on the oven to 350 °F.
2. In a small bowl, combine the oil, thyme, poultry seasoning, salt, and black pepper. Use the oil mixture to rub the turkey leg.
3. Put a small roasting pan with the turkey leg inside. Around the turkey leg in the roasting pan, pour the liquid. 1 hour and 40 minutes of roasting.
4. After removing the roasting pan from the oven, cover it with a piece of foil. 10 minutes should pass before serving..

Calories: 429 | Fat: 18.5g | Carbohydrates: 0.7g | Fiber: 0.1g | Sugar: 0g Protein: 51.6g | Sodium: 173mg

Turkey With Mushrooms

Prep Time: 10 minutes | Cook Time: 17 minutes | Serve: 1

Ingredients:

- Olive oil, 1/2 tablespoon
  - 1/4 pound of boneless, skinless turkey breast, sliced into 2-inch strips, 1 smashed garlic clove
  - 12 cup thinly sliced fresh mushrooms
  - 14 cup of chicken broth low in salt
  - 1 tablespoon tomato paste without sugar
    as needed, salt and freshly ground white pepper

Direction:

1. Sauté the garlic for about a minute in the oil that has been heated to medium heat in a nonstick skillet. Slices of turkey should be added now and cooked for 4–6 minutes. Transfer the turkey slices to a plate using a slotted spoon.
2. Add the mushrooms to the skillet and simmer for two to three minutes while stirring often. With intermittent stirring, simmer the broth for about 3–5 minutes after adding the tomato paste, salt, and pepper.
3. Slices of prepared turkey are added and heated for two to three minutes
4. Serve warm.

Calories: 219 | Fat: 7.7g | Carbohydrates: 5.4g | Fiber: 1.1g | Sugar: 2.6g Protein: 30.5g | Sodium: 246mg

Ground Turkey In Tomato Sauce

Prep Time: 10 minutes | Cook Time: 22 minutes | Serve: 1

Ingredients:

- Extra virgin olive oil, 1/2 tsp.
  - 14 of a chopped onion, 14 pounds of lean ground turkey
  - 12 of a minced garlic clove
  - 1/4 tsp. dried oregan
  - 1/4 cup tomato sauce without sugar
- 1 teaspoon chopped fresh parsley

Direction:

1. For about 5 minutes, sauté the onion in the oil in a small skillet over medium heat. Cook for about 6-7 minutes after adding the ground turkey, garlic, oregano, and red pepper flakes.
2. Add the tomato sauce, stir, and then cook for 8 to 10 minutes.
3. Serve hot with parsley as a garnish.

Calories: 252 | Fat: 14.5g | Carbohydrates: 5.16g | Fiber: 1.6g | Sugar: 3.3g Protein: 23.6g | Sodium: 309g

Ground Turkey with Pumpkin

Prep Time: 10 minutes | Cook Time: 30 minutes | Serve: 1

Ingredients:

- Extra virgin olive oil, 1/2 tsp.
- 1 finely sliced garlic clove and 1/4 of a small onion
- 14 pound of lean turkey ground
- 1 small tomato, coarsely chopped
- 3 ounces of pumpkin puree without sugar
- 14 teaspoon of cumin, ground
- a quarter-teaspoon of ground turmeric
- if needed, salt and freshly ground black pepper
- water, 1/4 cup

Direction:

1. For about five minutes, sauté the onion and garlic in oil in a skillet over medium-low heat. Cook the turkey for about 4 minutes after adding it. Cook the tomato for two to three minutes. Spices, water, and pumpkin puree are stirred together before being heated to a boil.
2. Stirring occasionally, lower the heat to medium-low, cover, and simmer for about 10-15 minutes.
3. Serve warm.

Calories: 281 | Fat: 13.5g | Carbohydrates: 10.1g | Fiber:4.6g | Sugar: 4.3g Protein: 24.3g | Sodium: 252mg

Duck Breast

Prep Time: 10 minutes | Cook Time: 16 minutes | Serve: 2

Ingredients:

- 1 finely sliced tiny shallot
- 1 teaspoon freshly minced ginger and 1/4 cup freshly chopped thyme
- if needed, salt and freshly ground black pepper
- 1 (12-ounce) breast of duck

Direction:

1. The shallot, ginger, thyme, salt, and black pepper should all be combined in a bowl. Duck breast should be added and evenly covered with marinade. Place in the refrigerator for 2 to 12 hours to marinate.
2. Set the grill's temperature to medium-high. Grease the grates on the grill.
3. Place the skin-side down on the grill and cook the duck breast for 6 to 8 minutes on each side.
4. Serve warm.

Calories: 229 | Fat: 6.9g | Carbohydrates: 2g | Fiber: 0.2g | Sugar: 0g Protein: 37.7g | Sodium: 79mg

Spiced Quail

Prep Time: 10 minutes | Cook Time: 31 minutes | Serve: 1

Ingredients:
- split into 1 tablespoons, 1/8 teaspoon ground cumin, and 1 pinch of ground coriander
- if needed, salt and freshly ground black pepper
- Cayenne pepper pinch
- 1 entire quail (514 ounces).
- 2 slices of lemo

Direction:
1. In a sizable baking dish, combine 14 tbsp of olive oil, cumin, coriander, salt, and black pepper. Place the quail there and thoroughly coat with oil mixture.
2. Put one slice of lemon in each quail's cavity. Tie the legs with kitchen thread.
3. In a sizable oven-safe wok, heat the remaining olive oil over high heat. Place the quail in the pan and cook for 2-4 minutes, or until golden brown, on each side.
4. Place the quail in the wok with the breast side facing up. Put a slice of lemon over each.

Calories: 412 | Fat: 17.5g | Carbohydrates: 0.3g | Fiber: 0.1g | Sugar: 0g Protein: 52.6g | Sodium: 156mg

Lemony Chicken Drumstick

Prep Time: 10 minutes | Cook Time: 40 minutes | Serve: 1

Ingredients:
- 1 skinless chicken drumstick, 1/4 cup extra virgin olive oil, and 1/4 cup lemon juice
- 14 teaspoon minced garlic
- 14 teaspoon grated lemon zest
- Italian seasoning, half a teaspoon
    as needed, salt and freshly ground white pepper

Direction:
1. In a sizable mixing bowl, combine oil, lemon juice, garlic, lemon zest, Italian seasoning, salt, and black pepper. Stir thoroughly. Add the chicken drumstick to the bowl and generously cover with the marinade. For at least 3-5 hours, cover the bowl and place in the fridge.
2. Turn on the oven to 400 °F. Cooking sheet greased.
3. Place the drumstick on the baking sheet that has been prepped. Bake for about 40 minutes, or until done as desired.
4. Serve warm.

Calories: 239 | Fat: 13.5g | Carbohydrates: 0.4g | Fiber: 0.1g | Sugar: 0.1g Protein: 25.2g | Sodium: 265mg

Fish Recipes

Baked Fish in Cream Sauce

Prep Time: 10 minutes Cooking Time: 40 minutes Servings: 4

Ingredients:

- 1 lb. haddock
- ½ cup all-purpose flour
- 2 tbsps. butter (unsalted)
- ¼ tsp. pepper
- 2 cups fat-free non-dairy creamer
- ¼ cup water

Direction:

1. your oven to 350 degrees Fahrenheit.
2. Spray oil on a baking sheet.
3. Add a small amount of flour.
4. Place fish in a pan.
5. Use pepper to season.
6. the fish with the remaining flour.
7. On both sides of the fish, apply creamer.
8. 40 minutes of baking or until golden.
9. Before serving, spread cream sauce over the fish.

Nutrition: Calories: 380 Protein: 23 g Carbohydrates: 46 g Fat: 11 g Cholesterol: 79 mg Sodium: 253 mg Potassium: 400 mg Phosphorus: 266 mg Calcium: 46 mg Fiber: 0.4 g

Shrimp & Broccoli

Prep Time: 10 minutes Cooking Time: 5 minutes Servings: 4

Ingredients:

- 1-tablespoon olive oil
- 1 minced garlic clove, 1 pound of shrimp
- Red bell pepper, 1/4 cup
- 1 cup steamed broccoli florets
- 10 ounces of cream cheese
- garlic powder, 1/2 tsp.
- Lemon juice, 1/4 cup
- 34 teaspoon of ground peppercorns
- quarter cup half-and-half cream

Direction:

1. Pour the oil into a pan and sauté the garlic for 30 seconds over medium heat.
2. Cook for 2 minutes after adding the shrimp.
3. Add the remaining components.
4. Mix well.
5. for two minutes.

Nutrition: Calories: 468 Protein: 27 g Carbohydrates: 28 g Fat: 28 g Cholesterol: 213 mg Sodium: 374 mg Potassium: 469 mg Phosphorus: 335 mg Calcium: 157 mg Fiber: 2.6 g

Shrimp in Garlic Sauce

Prep Time: 10 minutes Cooking Time: 6 minutes Servings: 4

Ingredients:

- 3 tablespoons butter (unsalted)
- 14 cup minced onion
- 3 minced garlic cloves
- 1 pound of shelled and deveined shrimp
- half a cup of half-and-half cream
- White wine, 1/4 cup
- Fresh basil, 2 tablespoons
- pepper to taste with black

Direction:

1. Add butter to a pan over medium-low heat.
2. Let it melt.
3. Add the onion and garlic.
4. Cook for 1 minute.
5. Add the shrimp and cook for 2 minutes.
6. Transfer shrimp on a serving platter and set aside.
7. Add the rest of the ingredients.
8. Simmer for 3 minutes.
9. Pour sauce over the shrimp and serve.

Nutrition: Calories: 483 Protein: 32 g Carbohydrates: 46 g Fat: 19 g Cholesterol: 230 mg Sodium: 213 mg Potassium: 514 mg Phosphorus: 398 mg Calcium: 133 mg Fiber: 2.0 g

Baked Trout

Prep Time: 5 minutes Cooking Time: 10 minutes Servings: 8

Ingredients:

- 2 lb. trout fillet
- 1 tbsp. oil
- 1 tsp. salt-free lemon pepper
- ½ tsp. paprika

Direction:

1. your oven to 350 degrees Fahrenheit.
2. Apply oil to the fillet.
3. Put the fish on the baking sheet.
4. Add paprika and lemon pepper to the seasoning.
5. For 10 minutes, bake.

Nutrition: Calories: 161 Protein: 21 g Carbohydrates: 0 g Fat: 8 g Cholesterol: 58 mg Sodium: 109 mg Potassium: 385 mg Phosphorus: 227 mg Calcium: 75 mg Fiber: 0.1 g

Broiled Shrimp

Prep Time: 10 minutes Cooking Time: 5 minutes Servings: 2

Ingredients:

- 1 lb. of shelled shrimp
- 2 teaspoons of lemon juice and melted 12 cup unsalted butter
- onion, chopped, 2 tablespoons
- 1 minced garlic clove
- pepper, 1/8 teaspoon

Direction:

1. In a bowl, combine the shrimp with the butter, lemon juice, onion, garlic, and pepper.
2. In a baking pan, spread the spiced shrimp.
3. Using the broiler setting in the oven, broil for 5 minutes.
4. Serve hot.

Nutrition: Calories: 164 Total Fat: 12.8 g Saturated Fat: 7.4 g Cholesterol: 167 mg Sodium: 242 mg Carbohydrates: 0.6 g Phosphorus: 215 mg Potassium: 228 mg

Grilled Lemony Cod

Prep Time: 10 minutes Cooking Time: 10 minutes Servings: 4

Ingredients:

- 1 lb. cod fillets
- 1 tsp. salt-free lemon pepper seasoning
- ¼ cup lemon juice

Direction:

1. Lemon juice and lemon pepper spice should be applied to the cod fillets.
2. Place the fish in a baking dish that has been sprayed with cooking oil.
3. In a preheated oven, bake the fish for 10 minutes at 350° F.
4. Serve hot.

Nutrition: Calories: 155 Total Fat: 7.1 g Saturated Fat: 1.1 g Cholesterol: 50 mg Sodium: 53 mg Carbohydrates: 0.7 g Calcium: 43 mg Phosphorus: 237 mg Potassium: 461 mg

Cucumber Bites, Smoked Salmon And Avocado

Prep time: 15 cooking Time: 10 minutes
Servings: 6

Ingredients:

- one large cucumber
- 1/8 teaspoon lime juice
- one huge avocado, peeled (pit removed)
- Chives
- Salmon smoked for six ounces
- roasted pepper

Direction:

1. Slice the cucumbers thinly, then distribute them evenly on a serving platter.
2. Avocado and lime juice should be combined in a cup and forked until frothy.
3. Each cucumber slice should have a tiny amount of avocado on it, and a thin slice of smoked salmon should be placed on top.
4. Cracked pepper and minced chives should be used to garnish each bite. Serve immediately..

Nutrition: Calories: 155 Total Fat: 7.1 g Saturated Fat: 1.1 g Cholesterol: 50 mg Sodium: 53 mg Carbohydrates: 0.7 g Calcium: 43 mg Phosphorus: 237 mg Potassium: 461 mg

Broiled Salmon Fillets

Prep Time: 10 minutes Cooking Time: 15 minutes Servings: 4

Ingredients:

- 1 tablespoon grated ginger root, 1 clove chopped garlic, and 1/4 cup maple syrup
- 1 tablespoon of spicy sauce
- 4 skinless salmon fillets

Direction:

1. Cooking spray-coated, set a pan over a moderate heat.
2. After 3 minutes of cooking, add the ginger and garlic and transfer to a bowl.
3. The ginger and garlic are combined with maple syrup and spicy sauce.
4. Mix thoroughly, then set this mixture aside.
5. The salmon fillet should be placed in a baking dish that has been coated with cooking oil.
6. generously spread the maple sauce over the fillets.
7. At broiler settings, bake them for ten minutes.
8. Serve hot.

Nutrition: Calories: 289 Total Fat: 11.1 g Saturated Fat: 1.6 g Cholesterol: 78 mg Sodium: 80 mg Carbohydrates: 13.6 g Phosphorus: 230 mg Potassium: 331 mg

Herbed Vegetable Trout

Prep Time: 10 minutes Cooking Time: 15 minutes Servings: 4

Ingredients:

- 15 trout fillets, 14 oz.
- 12 tsp. of herb seasoning mixture
- 1 sliced lemon
- 2 sliced green onions
- 1 sliced celery stalk
- julienned 1 medium carrot

Direction:

1. An open flame charcoal barbecue should be set up and heated.
2. Trout fillets should be spread out on a wide piece of foil with herb seasoning drizzled on top.
3. The fish should be covered with the lemon slices, carrots, celery, and green onions.
4. Wrap the fish with foil before packing it.
5. Cook the packed fish for 15 minutes on the grill.
6. Once finished, take the fish's foil off.
7. Serve.

Nutrition: Calories: 202 Total Fat: 8.5 g Saturated Fat: 1.5 g Cholesterol: 73 mg Sodium: 82 mg Carbohydrates: 3.5 g Phosphorus: 287 mg Potassium: 560 mg

Lemon Pepper Trout

Prep Time: 10 minutes Cooking Time: 15 minutes Servings: 2

Ingredients:

- Trout fillets, 1 pound
- 1 pound of asparagus
- 3 tablespoons olive oil
- 5 minced garlic cloves
- 1/2 teaspoon black pepper
- lemon, cut in half

Direction:

1. 350° F preparation and preheating of the gas oven.
2. After being cleaned, dried, and rubbed with oil, the fillets should be put in a baking dish.
3. Garlic cloves, lemon slices, and black pepper are sprinkled on top of the fish.
4. Around the fish, distribute the asparagus.
5. In the preheated oven, bake the fish for approximately 15 minutes.
6. Serve hot.

Nutrition: Calories: 336 Total Fat: 20.3 g Saturated Fat: 3.2 g Cholesterol: 84 mg Sodium: 370 mg Carbohydrates: 6.5 g Phosphorus: 107 mg Potassium: 383 mg

Fish With Mushrooms

Prep Time: 5 minutes Cooking Time: 16 minutes Servings: 4

Ingredients:

- 1 lb. cod fillet
- 2 tbsps. butter
- ¼ cup white onion, chopped
- 1 cup fresh mushrooms
- 1 tsp. dried thyme

Direction:

1. fresh sea scallops weighing 14 pound, side muscles removed
2. if needed, salt and freshly ground black pepper
3. Olive oil, 1/2 tablespoon
4. 14 teaspoon minced fresh parsley.

Nutrition: Calories: 155 Protein: 21 g Carbohydrates: 2 g Fat: 7 g Cholesterol: 49 mg Sodium: 110 mg Potassium: 561 mg Phosphorus: 225 mg Calcium: 30 mg

Parsley Scallops

Prep Time: 10 minutes | Cook Time: 7 minutes | Serve: 1

Ingredients:

- fresh sea scallops weighing 14 pound, side muscles removed
- if needed, salt and freshly ground black pepper
- Olive oil, 1/2 tablespoon
- 14 teaspoon minced fresh parsley

Direction:

1. The scallops should be salted and peppered.
2. The scallops should be cooked for two to three minutes on each side in a small skillet with the oil heated to medium-high heat.
3. After adding the parsley, turn off the heat.
4. Serve warm.

Calories: 160 | Fat: 7.9g | Carbohydrates: 2.7g | Fiber: 0g | Sugar: 0g Protein: 19.1g | Sodium: 238mg

Shrimp with Zucchini Noodles

Prep Time: 10 minutes | Cook Time: 7 minutes | Serve: 1

Ingredients:

- Olive oil, 1/2 tablespoon
- crushed red pepper flakes and half a tiny garlic clove, chopped
- Peeled and deveined medium shrimp weighing 14 pound
- if needed, salt and freshly ground black pepper
- Low-sodium chicken broth, 2 to 3 teaspoons
- Small zucchini cut in half and spiralized with Blade C
- 2-3 quartered cherry tomatoes

Direction:

1. Red pepper flakes and garlic are sautéed for about a minute in oil that has been heated in a small wok over medium heat. Cook shrimp for approximately a minute on each side after adding salt and black pepper.
2. Cook zucchini noodles in broth for two to three minutes. Add the tomatoes and stir after a minute.
3. Serve warm.

Calories: 211 | Fat: 9g | Carbohydrates: 4.8g | Fiber: 1g | Sugar: 1.6g Protein: 27g | Sodium: 248mg

Grilled Tilapia Tacos

Cooking + Prep Time: **30 minutes** Servings **4**

Ingredients:

- spray cans, olive oil
- 1/4 of a head of shreddable cabbage, little 8 x 6" soft tortillas, and corn
- a single garlic clove
- 2 tablespoons of fresh, chopped cilantro leaves
- chopped 1/4 cup red onion
- 4 chopped plum tomatoes
- 1 tablespoon of ancho chili powder
- 1 fresh lime wedge
- Canola oil, 2 sliced jalapenos, and 1/4 cup
- 4 x 4-oz. tilapia fillets, 1 pinch of salt, and sea

Direction:

1. Put the fish in the baking pan. Add three slices of lime juice to it. Fish is coated with chili powder, oil, and half of the jalapeno. Allow for roughly 15 minutes of marinating.
2. Combine lime juice, garlic, cilantro, onion, tomatoes, and the remaining jalapeño in a smaller bowl.
3. On medium-high, place a big skillet. Apply sea salt to the fish. Spray some cooking spray on the pan. Fill the pan with tilapia. For two minutes, cook. Cook for another minute after flipping.
4. Tortillas should be heated on the burner's eye over medium-high for 20 seconds on each side until lightly charred. Place a fillet half on each tortilla. Add salsa and cabbage as garnishes. Serve.

Calories from Fat 108. Calories 244. Total Fat 12g. Saturated Fat 4.1g

Tuna & Egg Salad

Prep Time: 10 minutes | Serve: 1

Ingredients:

- For Dressing
- ½ tablespoon fresh dill, minced
- ½ tablespoon olive oil
- ¼ tablespoon fresh lime juice
- Salt and ground black pepper, as required

    For Salad

- 1 cup fresh spinach, torn
- 3 ounces canned water-packed tuna, drained and flaked
- 1 hard-boiled egg, peeled and sliced
- ¼ cup tomato, chopped

Direction:

1. For dressing: place dill, oil, lime juice, salt, and black pepper in a small bowl and beat until well combined.
2. Place the spinach onto a serving plate and top with tuna, egg and tomato. Drizzle with dressing and serve.

Calories: 241 | Fat: 12.4g | Carbohydrates: 4.1g | Fiber: 1.4g | Sugar: 1.7g Protein: 28.8g | Sodium: 133mg

Shrimp & Olives Salad

Prep Time: 10 minutes | Cook Time: 3 minutes | Serve: 1

Ingredients:

- 14 pounds of peeled and deveined shrimp
- 1 slice of lemon
- Extra virgin olive oil, 1/2 tsp.
- 12 teaspoon of lemon juice, fresh
- if needed, salt and freshly ground black pepper
- 12 of a sliced tomato
- 1 tablespoon sliced onion
- green olives, 1 tbsp
- 1 teaspoon freshly chopped fresh parsley

Direction:

1. The lemon slice should be placed in a small pan of boiling, lightly salted water. The shrimp should then be added and cooked for two to three minutes, or until pink and opaque. To stop the cooking process, place the shrimp in a bowl of icy water using a slotted spoon. Completely drain the shrimp, then pat dry with paper towels.
2. The oil, lemon juice, salt, and black pepper should all be mixed thoroughly in a small dish with the oil.
3. On a serving plate, arrange the shrimp, tomato, onion, olives, and parsley. Serve after drizzling with the oil combination.

Calories: 215 | Fat: 9.9g | Carbohydrates: 4.5g | Fiber: 0.9g | Sugar: 1.3g Protein: 26.3g | Sodium: 305mg

Shrimp & Avocado Salad

Prep Time: 10 minutes | Serve: 1

Ingredients:

- Extra virgin olive oil, 1/2 tsp.
- 12 tablespoon lime juice, fresh
- 14 teaspoon of cumin, ground Add salt as needed.
- 14 lb. of cooked shrimp
- 12 a small avocado, cubed after being peeled and pitted
- Chopped scallion, half

Direction:

1. To make the dressing, put the oil, lime juice, cumin, and salt in a salad bowl.
2. Add the shrimp, avocado, and scallion to the salad bowl and gently stir to combine. Serve right away.

Calories: 285 | Fat: 15.5g | Carbohydrates: 7.5g | Fiber: 4.1g | Sugar: 0.5g Protein: 27.1g | Sodium: 237mg

Shrimp & Corn Salad

Prep Time: 10 minutes | Serve: 1

Ingredients:

- 14 lb. of cooked shrimp
- 1 cup of torn lettuce, 4 tablespoons of chopped onion
- a quarter cup of olive oil
- if needed, salt and freshly ground black pepper

Direction:

1. In a salad bowl, add shrimp, corn, onion, oil, salt and black pepper and toss to coat well.
2. Serve immediately.

Calories: 180| Fat: 5.5g | Carbohydrates: 5.1g | Fiber: 0.8g | Sugar: 1.4g Protein: 26.3g | Sodium: 236mg

Scallops & Tomato Salad

Prep Time: 10 minutes | Serve: 1

Ingredients:

- 1.5 pounds of cooked scallops
- 1 cup of young greens, mixed
- 14 cup halved grape tomatoes
- Olive oil, 1/2 tablespoon
- 12 tbsp of lemon juice, fresh
- if needed, salt and freshly ground black pepper

Direction:

1. In a salad bowl, add all the ingredients and stir to combine.
2. Serve immediately.

Calories: 173 | Fat: 8g | Carbohydrates: 5.1g | Fiber: 0.9g | Sugar: 1.7g Protein: 19.8g | Sodium: 245mg

Shrimp Lettuce Wraps

Prep Time: 10 minutes | Serve: 1

Ingredients:

- 14 lb. of cooked shrimp
- 1-2 teaspoons of finely chopped tomato
- 2 teaspoons chopped onion
- 1 teaspoon chopped fresh parsley
- 2 leaves of lettuce

Direction:

1. Combine shrimp, tomato, onion, and parsley in a bowl.
2. The lettuce leaves should be arranged on a serving plate. Over the lettuce leaves, evenly distribute the shrimp mixture.
3. Serve right away.

Calories: 149 | Fat: 2g | Carbohydrates: 4.9g | Fiber: 0.8g | Sugar: 1.6g Protein: 26.3g | Sodium: 280mg

Soup Recipes

Cauliflower & Pear Soup

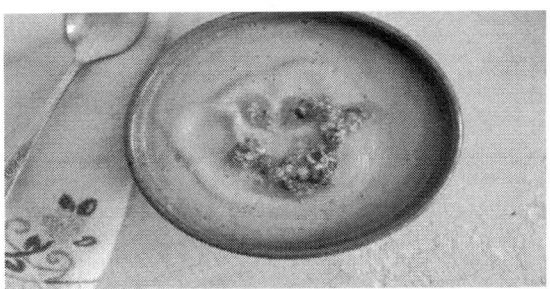

Prep Time: 15 min, cooking time: 30 min
Servings: 8

Ingredients:

- 750 g of cauliflower, 85 g of honey, 2 chopped pears, and 3 tablespoons of olive oil
- 3 sliced and peeled apples
- 1 carrot, diced, and 1 tablespoon minced garlic
- one sliced onion
- 1,400 liters of vegetable stock
- 2 tablespoons of clove powder
- 2 tablespoons chopped ginger
- 8 croutons for the decoration
- 2 tbsp alcohol from apple cider
- 6 fresh thyme sprigs

Direction:

1. Onions and carrots should be diced into medium-sized pieces, while cauliflower should be chopped into florets. Peeled and sliced into generous pieces, apples and pears should be prepared.
2. Cook pears and veggies in oil in a pan for around ten to fifteen minutes.
3. In a sizable mixing basin, combine the ginger, vegetable stock, cloves, cider, and apple cider vinegar. Bring to a boil, then simmer for 15 minutes on low heat. Add the herbs after adjusting the texture with more water or veggie broth. You can add croutons as a garnish and for their satisfying crunch. Enjoy.

Nutrition: Protein: 2.5 g, Fat: 5.8 g, Net Carbohydrates: 35.9 g

Chicken & Rice Soup

Prep Time: 10 min cooking time: 25 min
Servings: 8

Ingredients:

- Mirepoix, 375 g
- 50 g of finely chopped white onion and two diced celery sticks
- 245 g sliced baby carrots
- 155 grams of white rice, instant
- Olive oil extra virgin, 2 tablespoons
- 12 teaspoon black pepper
- Bay leaf, one
- 4 fresh thyme sprigs
- 1.5 tbsp lime juice
- 2 diced boneless chicken breasts
- Chicken and vegetable broth, 2.365 l

Direction:

1. Celery, onion, and carrot should be sautéed in olive oil until soft.
2. Rice, broth, bay leaf, fresh thyme, and pepper are all added to the saucepan. The mixture should boil.
3. Cook for around 15 minutes at the lowest heat setting.
4. Diced cooked chicken should be added. Ten minutes or so of low heat boiling.
5. Eliminate the bay leaf and add the lime juice..

Nutrition: Protein: 14 g , Fat: 3 g, Net Carbohydrates: 19 g

Corn and fennel soup

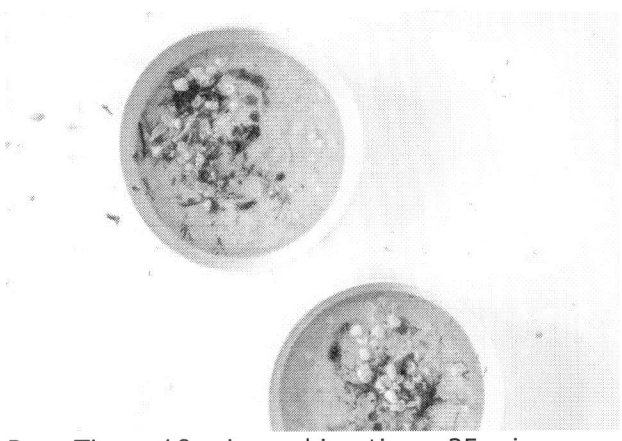

Prep Time: 10 min cooking time: 35 min
Servings: 12

Ingredients:

- shrimp shells
- 1 kg frozen corn
- 2 tbsp vegetable oil
- 2 onions/leeks, chopped
- 6 cloves of garlic
- 1 stick of celery, chopped
- Black pepper to taste
- 180 g chopped fennel
- 2 liters of cold water
- tarragon to taste

Direction:

1. Sauté shrimp shells in oil until they turn pink.
2. Sauté corn, onion, garlic, celery, and fennel until onions are translucent and flavor develops.
3. Bring the liquid to a boil and then remove from the heat.
4. Let simmer for at least 30 minutes.
5. Puree the soup until smooth, then filter to remove any remaining fibers.
6. Flavor with tarragon and fresh black pepper.

Nutrition: Protein: 3 g, fat : 3 g, Net Carbohydrates: 22 g

Thai fish soup

Prep Time: 15 min cooking time: 20 min
Servings: 12

Ingredients:

- Water, 1.180 l (boiling)
- Green onions, 10 g, chopped
- Whitefish, five fillets
- two minced garlic cloves
- Ginger, chopped, 1 tablespoon
- diced 130 g carrots
- basil
- Celery, 100 g, diced
- a pinch of coriander
- Bean sprouts 185 grams mint
- 100 grams of long grain rice (cooked)
- pepper flakes
- lime
- Chilies, dried (optional)

Direction:

1. Sweat the garlic, ginger, spring onions, and celery in a tablespoon of oil.
2. To the boiling water, add the fish, carrots, and celery.
3. Cook the fish until it's finished. Add black pepper and fresh herbs for seasoning.
4. Serve right away with the cooked rice.
5. Fresh herbs, bean sprouts, and additional lime juice are then added..

Nutrition: Protein: 3 g , Fat: 1.7 g, Net Carbohydrates: 10 g

Spring Pea Soup

Prep Time: 5 minutes Cooking Time: 15 minutes Servings: 6

Ingredients:
- 700 g of fresh peas, 2 tablespoons of coconut oil
- one small sliced onion
- broken-up mint leaves
- Vegetable stock, 1 liter
- Flat-leaf parsley, chopped
- juice of fresh lemons
- 12 tsp. cumin powder
- Celtic Sea salt, 2 teaspoons
- burnt sunflower seeds
- chopped nutmeg
- Black pepper powder, 1/2 tsp.

Direction:
1. In a pan over medium heat, warm the coconut oil.
2. Add the onions and stir-fry for 5 minutes or so.
3. Increase the heat after adding the stock. Cook fresh peas for 5 minutes after adding them. It should take half as long if you use frozen peas.
4. Add the salt, pepper, herbs, and spices, along with the lemon juice. agitating continuously
5. Before putting it through a food processor to the desired consistency, turn off the heat and let it cool.
6. Serve with mint or parsley leaves and sunflower seed garnish.
7. Enjoy!

Nutrition: Calories: 115 kcal Protein: 5 g Fat: 5.91 g Carbohydrates: 11.8 g

Canadian stew

Prep Time: 5 min Cooking Time: 8 hours Servings: 8

Ingredients:
- 500 grams of boneless beef
- 50 g of chopped onion
- 2/TBS of olive oil
- 6 peeled garlic cloves
- 260 g diced turnip
- Whole grain mustard, 1 tablespoon
- 310 g sliced carrots
- 945 ml of chicken or beef stock (low sodium)
- 355 g shredded cabbage

Direction:
1. In an oil-coated pan, sear the meat on all sides. Everything should be put in the slow cooker.
2. In the same pan, sauté chopped onion and garlic.
3. Stir the mustard into 8 ounces of beef/chicken stock after deglazing (low sodium). Continue filling the slow cooker with the remaining ingredients.
4. till beef is soft, about 8 hours on low. When necessary, season with salt and pepper.

Nutrition: Protein: 17 g, Fat: 8.7 g, Net Carbohydrates: 11 g

Shiitake broth

Prep Time: 5 min Cooking Time: 1-hour Servings: 4

Ingredients:

- 1.900L unsalted chicken and vegetable broth, 115 g fresh or dried shiitake mushrooms
- 2 tablespoons of ginger
- 4 entire spring onions
- 2 garlic cloves

Direction:

1. Add each ingredient to the pot. Heat to a simmer, then reduce to a low setting.
2. Cook for between 40 and 60 minutes at a low temperature.
3. Take out and save the liquid from the strainer. Place aside.

Nutrition: Protein: 1.4 g, Fat: 0.1 g, Net Carbohydrates: 9.4 g

Turkey Burger Soup

Prep time: 10 minutes cooking time: 25 minutes Servings: 4

Ingredients

- Olive oil, extra virgin, two tablespoons
- 1 lb. of turkey breast in ground form
- 12 a chopped sweet onion
- 3 minced garlic cloves
- black pepper freshly ground
- 1 (16-ounce) can of drained low-sodium diced tomatoes
- 4 cups of straightforward chicken broth or sodium-free store-bought chicken stock
- Sliced carrots in a cup
- 1 cup of celery, sliced
- 1 tablespoon freshly chopped basil
- 1 tablespoon freshly chopped oregano
- 1 tablespoon of freshly chopped thyme

Direction

1. Heat the olive oil in a medium stockpot over medium-high heat. Add the onion, garlic, and turkey. Cook and stir the turkey until it is well-browned. Use pepper to season.
2. Add the broth, carrots, celery, basil, oregano, and thyme along with the drained tomatoes. Stirring occasionally, simmer for 20 minutes on low heat. Serve.

Substitution tip: If you don't have fresh basil, oregano, or thyme, use dried instead. Substitute 1 teaspoon of dried herbs for each tablespoon of fresh.

Nutrition: Calories: 186 Fat: 11g Cholesterol: 26mg Carbohydrates: 17g Fiber: 3g Protein: 7g

Barbeque Sauce

Prep time: 15min, cook time: 20min, Serves: 8

Ingredients

- 1/2 cup tomato juice, 1/3 cup corn oil
- 1 - tbsp. brown sugar, one garlic clove
- 1 - tbsp. vinegar and 1/4 cup of paprika
- 1 - tsp. pepper and 1/3 cup of water. ¼ -tsp. garlic powder

Direction:

1. Consolidate all fixings first. About 20 minutes should be spent stewing.
2. After that, store any leftover portions in the refrigerator in a closed container..

Nutrition Facts: Calories 98g, Fat 4g, Carbs 13 g, Sugars 0.1g, Protein 22g

Basic Dressing

Prep time: 10min, cook time: 10min, Serves: 4

Ingredients

- Red wine vinegar, 1/4 cup, and 1/4 tsp. garlic powder
- 12 tsp. sugar, 14 tsp. dry mustard
- 1/4 cup water, 1/4 teaspoon black pepper
- 2 tablespoons of fresh lemon juice and 1 cup of corn

Direction:

1. First join all fixings and fill a holder with a tight-fitting top and shake well.
2. Then sore, shrouded in the fridge

Nutrition Facts: Calories 222g, Fat 18g, Carbs 5g, Sugars 2.3g, Protein 34g

Desert Recipes

Lemon ice cream torte

Prep Time: 5 min cooking time: 10 min
Servings: 1

Ingredients:

- water in 120 ml
- Light sour cream, 225 grams
- 1 little pack of flavorless gelatin
- Lemon juice, 60 ml
- Fat-Free Whipped Cream Topping, 575 g (Reddi-Wip)
- some lemon extract in a pinch
- 70g of sugar, granulated
- Cracker Pie Dough, 122 cm (Graham)
- Yellow food coloring, 6 drops

Direction:

1. 120 cc of hot water will help dissolve the gelatin. Give it five minutes to sit.
2. In a mixing dish, combine 460g of heavy cream with sugar, lemon juice, sour cream, lemon extract, and food coloring. Combine all of the ingredients. Add the dissolved gelatin and stir.
3. The ingredients should be placed halfway up the pie crust. Keep chilled until you're ready to use.
4. To serve, slice the cake into wedges and add a tablespoon of whipped cream to each wedge..

Nutrition: Eat Protein: 4 g, Fat:11 g, Net Carbohydrates: 35 g

Bagel bread pudding

Prep Time: 5 min, cooking time: 30 min,
Servings: 1

Ingredients:

- 1 medium baguette
- 60 g egg replacement (low cholesterol)
- a liter of almond milk
- 1 teaspoon of cinnamon
  Sugar 50 grams

Direction:

1. the oven to 170 °C.
2. Spray cooking spray in a small casserole dish.
3. Place the bagels on a baking sheet and break them apart.
4. In a mixing bowl, combine the egg replacement, almond milk, sugar, and cinnamon. Pour the mixture over the bagel pieces. Allow the bagels to soak up the liquid for a few minutes.
5. Bake for almost 30 minutes, or until golden brown on top. If desired, top with whipped cream.

Nutrition: Protein: 6 g , Fat: 2 g, Net Carbohydrates: 45 g

Mint Melted Chocolate Brownies

Prep Time: 5 min cooking time: 25-30 min
Servings: 12

Ingredients:

- 12 chocolates with mint
- brownie mix, one box
- Fresh mint sprigs, cocoa powder (unsweetened/sweetened), and powdered sugar (Optional Garnish)

Direction:

1. the oven to 180 C.
2. Start by making the brownie batter in accordance with the directions on the package. Use a 12-cup muffin tray, and lightly butter and flour the sides and bottom of the pan. Pour the brownie batter into the molds and bake for almost 25 minutes.
3. Place a slice of mint chocolate in the center of the brownies after taking them out of the oven, and bake for an additional 5 minutes. Turn off the oven after removing it. Give it five to ten minutes to cool.
4. Before serving, take the brownie cupcakes out of the pan.

Nutrition: Protein: 3 g , Fat: 22 g, Net Carbohydrates: 32 g

Saskatoon Berry Pudding

Prep Time: 5 min, cooking time: 40 min,
Servings: 6

Ingredients:

- 400 g fresh or frozen saskatoon berries
- 80g of sugar and 500 ml of water
- flour, 125 grams

Direction:

1. The fruit, sugar, and 12 ounces of water should all be combined in a medium pot.
2. Using a high heat, bring it to a boil.
3. Cook on a low setting for more than 30 minutes.
4. Flour should fill a small basin about halfway. To thoroughly combine, add 120ml of water.
5. Add the flour mixture to the berries and cook for 10 minutes on a low heat to thicken.

Nutrition: Protein: 2.1 g, Fat: 2.6 g, Net Carbohydrates: 32.9 g

Strawberries with balsamic vinegar and basil

Prep Time: 5 min cooking time: 10 min
Servings: 6

Ingredients:

- Sugar 50 grams
- 1 tablespoon of honey
- Balsamic vinegar, 60 g
- Freshly torn basil leaves, two tablespoons (small pieces)
- 12 teaspoon black pepper
- 12 an angel cake
- 500 g of strawberries, trimmed and cleaned (cut into small pieces)

Direction:

1. In a sizable mixing basin, combine the honey, sugar, pepper, and vinegar.
2. For brushing, mix in the strawberries and basil.
3. After covering, chill for at least 10 minutes and up to 1 1/2 hours.
4. Make six slices of the angel cake, then top each with 85g of chilled strawberries..

Nutrition: Protein: 2 g, Fat: 0 g, Net Carbohydrates: 34 g

Almond Meringue Cookies

Prep Time: 5 min cooking time: 25 min
Servings: 24 biscuits

Ingredients:

- 2 egg whites/ 4 tbsp. pasteurized egg white
- ½ tsp almond extract
- 1 tsp cream of tartar
- 100g of sugar
- ½ tsp vanilla extract

Direction:

1. Set the oven temperature to 150 °C.
2. Cream of tartar and egg whites should be mixed together until they have doubled in volume. Add the remaining ingredients and beat until stiff peaks form.
3. Press 1 teaspoon of meringue and 2 tablespoons of cookie batter onto the parchment-lined baking sheet using the back of another spoon.
4. The meringues should become crisp after roughly 25 minutes of baking at 150 °C. Keep the jar tightly closed.

Nutrition: Protein: 0.6 g, Fat: 3 g, Net Carbohydrates: 9 g

Apple Blueberry Crumb Cake

Prep Time: 15 min cooking time: 55 min
Servings: 8

Ingredients:

- 60 g of all-purpose flour, 60 g of brown sugar, and 310 g of rolled oats
- Margarine, 6 tbsp (90 gr.)
- 1 diced apple
- Blueberries, 200g
- 1.5 tbsp lemon juice

Direction:

1. Place the middle shelf in the oven and preheat it to 150 °C.
2. blend the dry In the mixing basin are the ingredients. Add the butter and stir until just moistened. Leave it alone.
3. Put brown sugar and rolled oats on a baking sheet that is 20 cm square. Fruit and lemon juice should be combined. Bake for approximately 55 to an hour, or until golden brown. hot or cold dishes.

Nutrition: Protein: 3.3 g, Fat: 12 g, Net Carbohydrates: 52 g

Raspberry Crumble Muffins

Prep Time: 10 min cooking time: 15-18 min
Servings: 16

Ingredients:

- 165g of flour and 220g of butter
- 1/2 a teaspoon of baking powder
- 120 grams raspberry fruit
- ½ egg
- liquid creamer, 100 g
- flour 35 grams
- Brown sugar, 50g
- 2/tsp. of cinnamon
- 2 tablespoons of margarine

Direction:

1. Pre-heat the oven to 190°C. Paper liners should be used to line a total of 16 muffin tins.
2. Mix the flour and baking powder in a small bowl. Embrace raspberries
3. Margarine should be thoroughly whipped with sugar and egg. With coffee creamer, blend. Add the flour mixture and stir until moistened. Prepare muffin tins.
4. Sprinkle the muffins with a mixture of brown sugar, cinnamon, and margarine from a small bowl. roughly 15–18 minutes of baking.

Nutrition: Protein: 5 g , Fat: 15 g, Net Carbohydrates: 50 g

Vanilla Custard

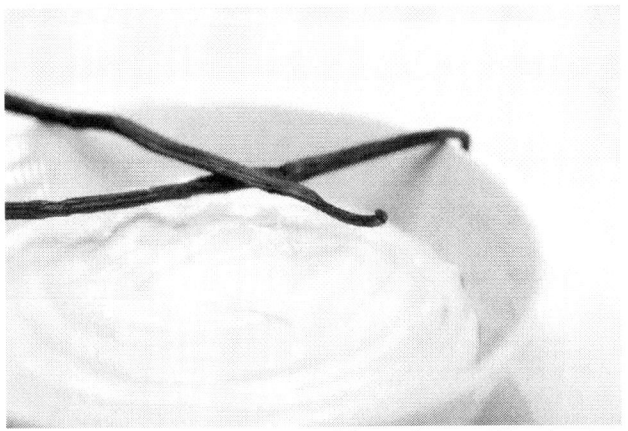

Prep time: 7 minutes cooking time: 10 minutes Servings: 10

Ingredients

- 1 egg, 1/8 tsp. vanilla extract
- 1/8 teaspoon of nutmeg
- 12 cup almond milk
- 2 tablespoons stevia.

Direction:

1. Milk should be somewhat cooled after being scalded.
2. In a bowl, crack the egg and stir in the nutmeg.
3. Add the vanilla, sweetener, and scalded milk as desired. Mix well.
4. Put the bowl in a baking pan with water that is 12 deep.
5. 30 minutes of baking at 325F.
6. Serve.

Nutrition: Calories: 167.3 Fat: 9g Carb: 11g Phosphorus: 205mg Potassium: 249mg Sodium: 124mg Protein: 10g

Bread Pudding

Prep time: 15 minutes cooking time: 40 minutes Servings: 6

Ingredients

- Unsalted butter, for greasing the baking dish
- Plain rice milk – 1 ½ cups
- Eggs – 2
- Egg whites – 2
- Honey – ¼ cup
- Pure vanilla extract – 1 tsp.
- Cubed white bread – 6 cups

Direction:

1. Butter an 8 by 8-inch baking dish and lightly oil it. Place aside.
2. The eggs, egg whites, rice milk, honey, and vanilla should all be combined in a bowl.
3. Bread cubes should be coated after adding them and stirring.
4. Place the mixture in the baking dish, then wrap it with plastic.
5. The dish should be kept in the fridge for at least three hours.
6. the oven to 325F for preheating.
7. Bake the pudding for 35 to 40 minutes, or until golden brown, after removing the plastic wrap from the baking dish.
8. Serve.

Nutrition: Calories: 167 Fat: 3g Carb: 30g Phosphorus: 95mg Potassium: 93mg Sodium: 189mg Protein: 6g

Strawberry Ice Cream

Prep time: 5 minutes cooking time: 5 minutes Servings: 3

Ingredients

- 12 cup of stevia
- 1 tablespoon of lemon juice
- 34 cup of nondairy coffee creamer
- Berry weight: 10 ounces
- ice, crushed: 1 cup

Direction:

1. Blend everything in a blend until smooth.
2. Freeze until frozen.
3. Serve.

Nutrition: Calories: 94.4 Fat: 6g Carb: 8.3g Phosphorus: 25mg Potassium: 108mg Sodium: 25mg Protein: 1.3g

Baked Peaches with Cream Cheese

Prep time: 10 minutes cooking time: 15 minutes Servings: 4

Ingredients

- 1 cup of plain cream cheese, 1/2 cup of crushed meringue cookies, and 1/4 teaspoon of ground cinnamon
- pinch of nutmeg, ground
- 8 peach halves in juice from cans
- 2 Tbsp. of honey.

Direction:

1. Set the oven to 350 degrees.
2. Use parchment paper to cover a baking sheet. Place aside.
3. The meringue cookies, cream cheese, cinnamon, and nutmeg should all be combined in a small basin.
4. Fill the cavities in the peach halves evenly with the cream cheese mixture.
5. Bake the peaches for 15 minutes, or until they are tender and the cheese is melted, on the baking sheet.
6. Peaches should be taken off the baking sheet and placed on plates.
7. Serve with a honey glaze.

Nutrition: Calories: 260 Fat: 20g Carb: 19g Phosphorus: 74mg Potassium: 198mg Sodium: 216mg Protein: 4g

Gingerbread-muffins

Prep time: 5 min, cooking time: 25 min, Servings: 1

Ingredients:
- 2 eggs
- Canola oil, 6 tbsp.
- 180 ml of 1% low-fat milk
- Dark corn syrup, 4 teaspoons
- Brown sugar 100g
- 1-tablespoon baking powder
- 4 teaspoons ground ginger
- All-purpose flour, 300 grams
- two teaspoons of cinnamon

Direction:
1. the oven to 170 °C.
2. In a 12-cup muffin tray, grease and insert paper liners.
3. In a mixing dish, whisk the eggs just a little bit. Combine the milk, corn syrup, brown sugar, and oil in a bowl.
4. In a mixing basin, combine the baking powder, flour, cinnamon, and ginger. Fill the well in the middle of the dry ingredients with the liquid ingredients. Stir very slowly until just combined
5. Half the batter should go into each muffin cup. Cook for roughly 20 minutes in a preheated oven until golden brown and yet firm to the touch.
6. After removing the muffins from the oven, give them about five minutes to cool in the pan. Include a dab of butter or cream cheese when serving..

Nutrition: Protein: 4 g, Fat: 8 g, Net Carbohydrates: 32 g

Zucchini Brownies

Prep time: 15 min, cooking time: 30-35 min, Servings: 16

Ingredients:
- Wholemeal flour, 130 grams
- 55 grams of cocoa butter
- 2 eggs, 100g of oat bran
- Baking powder, 1/2 tsp.
- Ground flaxseed, 25 g
- Brown sugar 100g
- Rapeseed oil in 80 ml
- 250 grams of plain applesauce
- grated tiny courgettes, 175 g
- 1 teaspoon vanilla extract
- 90 g pieces of dark chocolate

Direction:
1. the oven to 180 degrees Celsius. Clean and grease a 28 x 20 cm baking pan.
2. Oat bran, flour, flaxseed, baking powder, and cocoa are all combined in a mixing bowl.
3. In another bowl, combine the oil and sugar. Add eggs, vanilla essence, and applesauce. Completely combine. blend the dry components, and stir in. Zucchini that has been grated and chocolate chips should also be added. The batter will be thick.
4. Half-fill the baking pan with batter, then use a spatula to level the top. Bake for about 30 minutes on the center shelf. After letting cool fully, cut into 16 pieces.

Nutrition: Protein: 4 g , Fat: 9 g, Net Carbohydrates: 24 g

Strawberries with balsamic vinegar and basil

Prep time: 5 min cooking time: 10 min
Servings: 6

Ingredients:

- Sugar 50 grams
- 1 tablespoon of honey
- Balsamic vinegar, 60 g
- Freshly torn basil leaves, two tablespoons (small pieces)
- 12 teaspoon black pepper
- 12 an angel cake
- 500 g of strawberries, trimmed and cleaned (cut into small pieces)

Direction:

1. In a sizable mixing basin, combine the honey, sugar, pepper, and vinegar.
2. For brushing, mix in the strawberries and basil.
3. After covering, chill for at least 10 minutes and up to 1 1/2 hours.
4. Make six slices of the angel cake, then top each with 85g of chilled strawberries.

Nutrition: Protein: 2 g, Fat: 0 g, Net Carbohydrates: 34 g

Raspberry Cheesecake Mousse

Prep time: 5 min cooking time: 15 min
Servings: 6

Ingredients:

- 1 12 cups celery, 12 cups chicken
- 1/4 cup of thinly sliced onion and 1/2 cup of green pepper
- Mandarin orange segments in a cup, along with 1/4 cup of light mayo
- 1/2 teaspoon of freshly ground pepper.

Direction:

1. Cream cheese and 100 g sugar should be frothy after being combined. Add lemon zest and vanilla extract. For decoration, set aside a few raspberries. The remaining raspberries should be mashed with a fork before adding the melted sweetener. Gently but quickly incorporate the mashed raspberries into the cream cheese batter after continuing to whisk in the light whipping cream.
2. Mousse should be poured into six presentation glasses halfway, then chilled until ready to serve.
3. Before serving, garnish the mousse with fresh raspberries and a sprig of crisp mint.

Nutrition: Protein: 3 g, Fat: 15 g, Net Carbohydrates: 29 g

Salad Recipes

Chicken and Mandarin Salad

Prep time: 40min, cook time: 30min, Serves: 3

Ingredients

- 1 12 cups of chicken, 12 cups of celery
- 1/2 cup green pepper and 1/4 cup thinly sliced onion
- 1 cup of segments of Mandarin oranges and 1/4 cup of light mayonnaise
- freshly ground pepper, 1/2 tsp.

Direction:

1. First hurl chicken, celery, green pepper and onion to blend.
2. Then include mandarin oranges, mayo and pepper. Blend delicately and serve.

Nutrition: Calories 365g, Fat 16g, Carbs 13g, Sugars 0.4g, Protein 29g

Tuna macaroni salad

Prep time: 5 minutes cooking time: 25 minutes
Servings: 10 servings

Ingredients:

- 1 and a half cups raw macaroni
- 1 170g tuna in water can
- Mayonnaise, 1/4 cup
- chopped celery from two medium stalks
- Lemon Pepper Seasoning, 1 tablespoon

Direction:

1. Pasta that has been cooked should be refrigerated to cool.
2. Tuna should be rinsed with cold water after being drained in a colander.
3. When the macaroni has cooled, include the tuna and celery.
4. Add the mayonnaise and season with the lemon after stirring. Mix well. Offer chilled.

Nutrition: Power: 136 g, Protein: 8.0 g, Carbohydrates: 18 g, fibbers: 0.8 g, Fat: 3.6 g, Sodium: 75 mg, Potassium: 124 mg, Phosphorus: 90 mg

Fruity zucchini salad

Prep time: 5 minutes cooking time: 5 minutes
Servings: 4 servings

Ingredients:

- 400 g of zucchini
- 1 little onion
- 4 tablespoons of extra virgin olive oil
- 100g drained pineapple preserves
- paprika, salt
- thyme

Direction:

1. The onions should be diced and cooked in oil until transparent.
2. Slice the zucchini, then include. Add salt, paprika, and thyme for seasoning.
3. Mix with the diced pineapple after cooling.

Nutrition: Energy: 150kcal, Protein: 2g, Fat: 10g, Carbohydrates: 10g, Dietary fibbers: 2g, Potassium: 220mg, Calcium: 38mg, Phosphate: 24mg

Hawaiian Chicken Salad

Prep time: 5 minutes cooking time: 30 minutes
Servings: 4

Ingredients:

- 1 1/2 cups of cooked, chopped chicken breast
- 1 cup of chunky pineapple
- 1 1/4 cups shredded iceberg lettuce
- chopped celery in a half cup
- 50 ml of mayonnaise
- Tabasco sauce, 1/8 teaspoon (dash).
- Lemon juice, two
- Black pepper, 1/4 teaspoon

Direction:

1. In a medium bowl, mix the cooked chicken, pineapple, lettuce, and celery. Simply set aside.
2. Make the dressing in a small bowl. Combine the lemon juice, pepper, Tabasco sauce, and mayonnaise.
3. Add the dressing to the chicken mixture and whisk to combine.

Nutrition: Power: 310 g, Protein: 16.8 g, Carbohydrates: 9.6 g, fibbers: 1.1 g, Fat: 23.1 g, Sodium: 200 mg, Potassium: 260 mg, Phosphorus: 134 mg

Macaroni Salad

Prep time: 5 minutes Cooking time: 5 minutes
Servings: 4

Ingredients:

- 1/4 teaspoon celery seed
- two boiled eggs
- a salad dressing of two cups
- 1 onion
- White vinegar, two teaspoons
- Celery stalks, two
- cooked macaroni, two cups
- one red pepper
- 2 tablespoons mustard

Direction:

1. In a bowl add all ingredients and mix well
2. Serve with dressing

Nutrition: Calories 360, Fat 21g, Sodium (Na) 400mg, Carbs 36g, Protein 6g, Potassium (K) 68mg, Phosphorus 36 mg

Grapes Jicama Salad

Prep Time: 5 minutes Cooking Time: 0 minutes
Servings: 2

Ingredients:

- 1 sliced and peeled jicama
- 1 sliced carrot and 1/2 a medium red onion
- Grapes, seedless, 1 1/4 cups
- 1/3 cup of basil leaves, fresh
- 1 teaspoon vinegar made from apple cider
- 1 1/2 teaspoons of lemon juice
- 1 1/2 teaspoons of lime juice

Direction:

1. In a good salad bowl, combine the salad's components.
2. Give them a good toss and chill for an hour.
3. Serve.

Nutrition: Calories 203 Total Fat 0.7g Sodium 44mg Protein 3.7g Calcium 79mg Phosphorous 141mg Potassium 429mg

Italian Cucumber Salad

Prep Time: 5 minutes Cooking Time: 0 minutes
Servings: 2

Ingredients:

- rice vinegar, 1/4 cup
- 1/eight teaspoon
- 50 ml of olive oil
- black pepper, 1/8 teaspoon
- sliced cucumbers, half
- 1 cup sliced carrots
- 2 teaspoons thinly sliced green onions
- 2 tablespoons of thinly sliced red bell pepper
- 1/3 of an Italian seasoning mixture teaspoon

Direction:

1. Put all the salad ingredients into a suitable salad bowl.
2. Toss them well and refrigerate for 1 hour.
3. Serve.

Nutrition: Calories 112 Total Fat 1.6g Cholesterol 0mg Sodium 43mg Protein 2.3g Phosphorous 198mg Potassium 529mg

Barb's Asian Slaw

Prep Time: 5 minutes Cooking Time: 5 minutes
Servings: 2

Ingredients:

- 1 cabbage head, shredded
- 4 chopped green onions
- ½ cup slivered or sliced almonds

  Dressing:

- ½ cup olive oil
- ¼ cup tamari or soy sauce
- 1 tablespoon honey or maple syrup
- 1 tablespoon baking stevia

Direction:

1. Heat up dressing ingredients in a saucepan on the stove until thoroughly mixed.
2. Mix all ingredients when you are ready to serve.

Nutrition: Calories: 205 Protein: 27g Carbohydrate: 12g Fat: 10 g Calcium 29mg, Phosphorous 76mg, Potassium 27mg Sodium: 111 mg

Green Bean and Potato Salad

Prep Time: 5 minutes Cooking Time: 5 minutes
Servings: 4

Ingredients:

- Basil, 1/2 cup
- Olive oil, 1/4 cup
- a teaspoon of mustard
- 1/4 lb. of green beans
- one teaspoon of lemon juice
- Balsamic vinegar, 1/2 cup
- red onion, 1
- 1 pound of red carrots
- 1 clove of garlic

Direction:

1. When the carrots are soft, place them in a pot with water and bring to a boil for 15 to 18 minutes.
2. Green beans can be added after 5 to 6 minutes.
3. Drain and cube the food.
4. Combine all ingredients in a bowl.
5. With dressing, serve

Nutrition: Calories 153.2, Fat 2.0 g, Sodium 77.6 mg, Potassium 759.0 mg, Carbs 29.0 g, Protein 6.9 g, Phosphorus 49 mg

Pear & Brie Salad

Prep Time: 5 minutes Cooking Time: 0 minutes
Servings: 4

Ingredients:

- Olive oil, 1 tbsp
- 1/2 lemon and 1 cup arugula
- 12 cup of pears in cans
- 1/4 cucumber
- chopped 1/4 cup brie

Direction:

1. Slice the cucumber into dice.
2. Dice the pears.
3. Clean the arugula.
4. In a serving bowl, combine the salad ingredients and sprinkle the brie on top.
5. Lemon juice and olive oil are combined by whisking.
6. over the salad, drizzle.
7. Serve right away after adding some black pepper to taste.

Nutrition: Calories 54, Protein 1 g, Carbs 12 g, Fat 7 g, Sodium 57mg, Potassium 115 mg, Phosphorus 67 mg

Caesar Salad

Prep Time: 5minutes Cooking Time: 5minutes
Servings: 4

Ingredients:

- 1 head of lettuce, romaine
- Mayonnaise, 1/4 cup
- one teaspoon of lemon juice
- Anchovy fillets, four
- Worcestershire sauce, one teaspoon
- roasted pepper
- 5 cloves of garlic
- four tablespoons Camembert cheese
- 1 tablespoon of mustard

Direction:

1. In a bowl mix all ingredients and mix well
2. Serve with dressing

Nutrition: Calories 44, Fat 2.1 g, Sodium 83 mg, Potassium 216 mg, Carbs 4.3 g, Protein 3.2 g, Phosphorus 45.6mg Calcium 19mg, Potassium 27mg Sodium: 121 mg

Thai Cucumber Salad

Prep Time: 5minutes Cooking Time: 5minutes
Servings: 2

Ingredients:

- Peanuts, chopped, 14 cup
- White sugar, 1/4 cup
- 12 cup of cilantro
- Rice wine vinegar, 1/4 cup
- three cukes
- Jalapeno peppers, two

Direction:

1. Add all ingredients in a small basin and combine well
2. Serve with dressing

Nutrition: Calories 20, Fat 0g, Sodium 85mg, Carbs 5g, Protein 1g, Potassium 190.4 mg, Phosphorus 46.8mg

Vegetarian Recipes

Cream Cheese Herb Toasts

Prep time: 15 min cooking time: 0 min
Servings: 5

Ingredients:

- Toast with mlb
- Soft cream cheese 180 grams
- 1 clove of garlic (halved)
- 2 tablespoons chopped onion or shallot
- 5g of chopped mixed herbs, including dill, tarragon, chives, parsley, and thyme
- 2 tablespoons of water
- 12 teaspoon black pepper

Direction:

1. Mix the herbs, cream cheese, pepper, shallot, and water in a medium bowl until smooth.
2. With the cut edge of the garlic clove, rub the bread.
3. Toast with cream cheese spread on it is served.

Nutrition: Protein: 2.6 g, Fat: 1 g, Net Carbohydrates: 10 g

Aubergine puree

Prep time: 5 min cooking time: 20 min
Servings: 4

Ingredients:

- 1 kilogram of abergas (pricked with a fork and washed)
- Tahini, 30 ml
- 2/TBS of olive oil
- 1 peeled garlic clove
- Juiced lemon, one
- 12 teaspoon of salt

Direction:

1. On a gas stove, cook each eggplant for 5 minutes before rotating. The auberges ought to be completely cooked and completely black all over after 20 to 30 minutes.
2. The pan should be taken off the heat and left to cool completely.
3. Blend the auberges and the remaining ingredients in a food processor until smooth.
4. Serve and enjoy with breadsticks, flatbread, or raw veggies as a snack, as part of a substantial meal, a lighter lunch, or as part of a larger meal.

Nutrition: Protein : 2 g, Fat: 3.5 g, Net Carbohydrates: 7.7 g

Vegan Pie (White Bean Spread)

Prep time: 10 min cooking time: 2 min
Servings: 2

Ingredients:

- 1 small onion
- 2/TBS of olive oil
- a single garlic clove
- Sun-dried tomatoes, 15 grams (in oil)
- 440g of white beans in cans
- 2 tbsp. chopped fresh or frozen parsley (use less if dried)
- ½ lemon (squeezed)
- 1 teaspoon water
- 2 tablespoons chopped fresh or frozen chives
- pepper and salt as desired

Direction:

1. Chop the onion and garlic roughly.
2. They should be lightly browned after a few minutes of frying in oil. Once ready, combine the two ingredients in the mixing bowl. Place the beans in the basin after draining and washing.
3. You should squeeze the lemon.
4. In a hand mixer, thoroughly combine the other Ingredients with the lemon juice. Alternately, combine everything and place it in the processor. if desired, serve with warmed whole wheat bread. you like.

Nutrition: Protein: 13 g , Fat: 16 g, Net Carbohydrates: 42 g

Simple Roasted Broccoli

Prep Time: 5 Minutes Cooking Time: 20 Minutes
Serving: 6

Ingredients:

- 2 little heads of floretized broccoli
- Extra virgin olive oil, 1 tablespoon
- 3 minced garlic cloves

Direction:

1. Set the oven to 425 °F.
2. Combine the broccoli, garlic, and olive oil in a medium bowl. Place on a baking sheet in a single layer.
3. 3Roast the broccoli for 10 minutes, flip it over, and roast for an additional 10 minutes. Serve.

Cooking tip: Roasted broccoli makes for great leftovers—throw them in a quick salad for added flavor and bulk. To save leftovers, refrigerate in an airtight container for three to five days.

Nutrition Per Serving Calories: 38; Total Fat: 2g; Saturated Fat: 0g; Cholesterol: 0mg; Carbohydrates: 4g; Fiber: 1g; Protein: 1g; Phosphorus: 32mg; Potassium: 150mg; Sodium: 15mg

Roasted Mint Carrots

Prep Time: 5 Minutes Cooking Time: 20 Minutes Serving: 6

Ingredients:

- 1 pound of cut carrots
- Extra virgin olive oil, 1 tablespoon
- black pepper freshly ground
- 14 cup of mint, finely cut

Direction:

1. Set the oven to 425 °F.
2. On a baking sheet with a rim, spread out the carrots in a single layer. Sprinkle the carrots on the sheet with the olive oil and shake to coat. Use pepper to season.
3. Roast for 20 minutes, stirring twice during cooking, or until fork-tender and browned. Add the mint and then serve.
   Substitution tip: To lower the potassium in this dish, use 8 ounces of carrots and 8 ounces of turnips cut into cubes. This will cut the potassium to 193mg.

Nutrition Per Serving Calories: 51; Total Fat: 2g; Saturated Fat: 0g; Cholesterol: 0mg; Carbohydrates: 7g; Fiber: 2g; Protein: 1g; Phosphorus: 26mg; Potassium: 242mg; Sodium: 52mg

Roasted Asparagus

Prep Time: 5 minutes Cooking Time: 10 minutes Servings: 4

Ingredients:

- Extra virgin olive oil, 1 tablespoon
- 100 grams of fresh asparagus
- zested 1 medium lemon
- freshly grated nutmeg, 1/2 teaspoon
- Kosher salt, 1/2 teaspoon
  1/2 teaspoon black pepper

Direction:

1. Set the oven to 500 degrees Fahrenheit.
2. Add extra virgin olive oil and asparagus to a sheet of aluminum foil.
3. Prepare the asparagus in a single layer, then fold the foil's edges.
4. Cook for five minutes in the oven. Roasting should continue until browned.
5. Before serving, incorporate the roasted asparagus with the nutmeg, salt, zest, and pepper.

Nutrition: Calories: 55 Fat: 3.8 g Carbs: 4.7 g Protein: 2.5 g Sodium: 98mg Potassium: 172mg Phosphorus: 35mg

Vinegar & Salt Kale

Prep Time: 10 minutes Cooking Time: 12 minutes Servings: 2

Ingredients:

- 1 head of chopped kale
- Extra virgin olive oil, 1 teaspoon
- 1 teaspoon vinegar made from apple cider
- Sea salt, 1/2 teaspoon

Direction:

1. In a bowl, combine the chopped kale with the vinegar and extra virgin olive oil.
2. After salting, use your hands to knead the ingredients.
3. On two baking pans coated with parchment paper, spread out the kale and bake until crispy for about 12 minutes at 375°F.
4. 10 minutes should pass for cooling before serving.

Nutrition: Calories: 152 Fat: 8.2 g Carbs: 15.2 g Protein: 4 g Sodium: 170mg Potassium: 304mg Phosphorus: 37mg

Lemony Brussels Sprout

Prep Time: 10 minutes | Cook Time: 15 minutes | Serve: 1

Ingredients:

- fresh Brussels sprouts, cut in half and trimmed, 14 pound.
- Olive oil, 1/2 tablespoon
- 12 of a minced garlic clove
- Crushed red pepper flakes in a pinch
- if needed, salt and freshly ground black pepper
- 12 teaspoon of lemon juice, fresh

Direction:

1. Over a sizable pan of boiling water, place a steamer basket. Put the Brussels sprouts in the steamer basket and steam them for 6 to 8 minutes with the lid on. Remove the Brussels sprouts from the heat and thoroughly drain them.
2. The garlic and red pepper flakes should be sautéed for about a minute in oil that has been heated to medium heat in a wok. Sauté the Brussels sprouts for around 4-5 minutes after adding salt and black pepper. Add the lemon juice, stir, and cook for an additional 30 seconds.
3. Serve warm.

Calories: 113 | Fat: 7.5g | Carbohydrates: 10g | Fiber: 3.4g | Sugar: 2.5g Protein: 4g | Sodium: 176mg

Simple Asparagus

Prep Time: 5 minutes | Cook Time: 5 minutes | Serve: 1

Ingredients:

- 14 pound of trimmed asparagus and 14 tablespoon of olive oil
- if needed, salt and freshly ground black pepper

Direction:

1. Cook the asparagus for 3 to 5 minutes in a pan of water.
2. Transfer the asparagus to a dish after draining. Add some oil, salt, and black pepper, and drizzle.
3. Serve warm.

Calories: 53 | Fat: 3.6g | Carbohydrates: 4.4g | Fiber: 2.4g | Sugar: 2.1g Protein: 2.5g | Sodium: 157mg

Gingered Asparagus

Prep Time: 10 minutes | Cook Time: 6 minutes | Serve: 1

Ingredients:

- a quarter cup of olive oil
- 1/4 tsp. cumin seed
- fresh asparagus weighing 1/4 pound, trimmed, and sliced into 2-inch diagonal sections.
- 14 teaspoon minced fresh ginger
- 1/4 teaspoon of lemon juice, fresh
- if needed, salt and freshly ground black pepper

Direction:

1. Cumin seeds should be sautéed for about a minute in oil heated over medium heat in a small non-stick skillet. Stir-fry the remaining ingredients for 4-5 minutes after adding them.
2. Serve warm.

Calories: 60 | Fat: 3.9g | Carbohydrates: 5.6g | Fiber: 2.6g | Sugar: 2.2g Protein: 2.7g | Sodium: 159mg

Balsamic Asparagus

Prep Time: 10 minutes | Cook Time: 10 minutes | Serve: 1

Ingredients:

- 1/4 cup balsamic vinegar, 1/4 teaspoon chopped garlic, and 1/2 tablespoon olive oil
- 14 teaspoon chopped fresh parsley
- 1/4 tsp. dried oregano
- if needed, salt and freshly ground black pepper
- fresh asparagus, 4 ounces, ends cut off.

Direction:

1. Turn on the oven to 400 °F. Lightly grease a baking sheet with a rim.
2. Oil, lemon juice, vinegar, garlic, herbs, salt, and black pepper should all be mixed thoroughly in a bowl with the oil.
3. Place asparagus in a single layer on the baking sheet that has been prepared. Add the herb mixture on top and coat with a toss. Approximately 8 to 10 minutes for roasting.
4. Serve warm.

Calories: 86 | Fat: 7.2g | Carbohydrates: 5g | Fiber: 2.6g | Sugar: 2.2g Protein: 2.6g | Sodium: 155mg

Spiced Mushrooms

Prep Time: 10 minutes | Cook Time: 15 minutes | Serve: 1

Ingredients:

- Olive oil, 1/2 tablespoon
- 1/4 teaspoon cumin seeds, finely crushed 1/4 thinly sliced yellow onion
- 14 pound of chopped white button mushrooms
- 1/4 teaspoon of coriander, ground
- Garam masala powder, 1/4 teaspoon
- Red chili powder, 1/4 teaspoon
- 1/8 teaspoon of turmeric powder Salt, as needed
- 1 teaspoon minced fresh cilantro leaves

Direction:

1. Cumin seeds should be sautéed for about a minute in oil heated over medium heat. For about 4 minutes, add the onion and continue to sauté. Sauté the mushrooms for 5 to 7 minutes after adding them. For around 1-2 minutes, add the salt and spices and sauté.
2. Add the cilantro and cook for a further 30 seconds. Serve warm

Calories: 100 | Fat: 7.6g | Carbohydrates: 7.1g | Fiber: 2.1g | Sugar: 3.2g Protein: 4.1g | Sodium: 161mg

Parsley Mushrooms

Prep Time: 10 minutes | Cook Time: 15 minutes | Serve: 1

Ingredients:

- Olive oil, 1/2 tablespoon
- 1 tablespoon finely minced yellow onion 1/4 pound finely chopped white button mushrooms
- if needed, salt and freshly ground black pepper
- 2 tablespoons chopped fresh parsley

Direction:

1. For around 4-5 minutes, sauté the onion in oil in a wok over medium heat. Sauté the mushrooms for 5 to 7 minutes after adding them. Sauté for about 1-2 minutes after adding the salt and black pepper.
2. Add the parsley and continue to sauté for about another minute.
3. Serve warm.

Calories: 89 | Fat: 7.4g | Carbohydrates: 4.8g | Fiber: 1.4g | Sugar: 2.4g Protein: 3.8g | Sodium: 163mg

Mushroom With Spinach

Prep Time: 10 minutes | Cook Time: 15 minutes | Serve: 1

Ingredients:

- 1/3 cup extra virgin olive oil
- 1 clove of finely minced garlic and 1/4 of an onion
- 3 ounces of chopped, fresh button mushrooms
- 4 ounces of chopped fresh spinach
- 14 teaspoon of cumin, ground
- if needed, salt and freshly ground black pepper

Direction:

1. For around four to five minutes, sauté the onion and garlic in oil in a saucepan over medium heat. Add the mushroom to the stir-fry and cook for 5 to 6 minutes. Cook for 3–4 minutes before adding salt, black pepper, cumin, and spinach.
2. Serve warm.

Calories: 95 | Fat: 5.4g | Carbohydrates: 9.7g | Fiber: 3.4g | Sugar: 3g Protein: 5.6g | Sodium: 230mg

Herbed Cauliflower

Prep Time: 10 minutes | Cook Time: 20 minutes | Serve: 1

Ingredients:

- Cauliflower florets, 1/4 cup
- 1 tiny, peeled, and halved garlic clove
- Olive oil, 1/2 tablespoon
- 1/4 cup fresh lemon juice
- 1/8 teaspoon crushed dried thyme
- 1/8 teaspoon crumbled dried oregano
- if needed, salt and freshly ground black pepper

Direction:

1. Turn on the oven to 425 °F. Grease a baking dish liberally.
2. Add all the ingredients to a glass bowl and toss to evenly coat.
3. Spread the cauliflower mixture in a single layer in the baking dish that has been prepared. Roast for about 15-20 minutes, stirring twice, or to the desired doneness.
4. Serve warm.

Calories: 73 | Fat: 7.1g | Carbohydrates: 2.6g | Fiber: 0.8g | Sugar: 0.7g Protein: 0.8g | Sodium: 164mg

Garlicky Broccoli

Prep Time: 10 minutes | Cook Time: 9 minutes | Serve: 1

Ingredients:

- 1/3 cup extra virgin olive oil
- 1/2 cup of broccoli florets and 1 minced garlic clove
- low-sodium soy sauce in a tablespoon
- Red pepper flakes with a pinch

Direction:

1. The garlic should be sautéed in the oil for about a minute over medium heat in a small non-stick skillet. Stir-fry the broccoli for two to three minutes after adding it. Stir fried for around 4-5 minutes after adding the soy sauce.
2. Serve warm.

Calories: 66 | Fat: 4.9g | Carbohydrates: 5.1g | Fiber: 1.3g | Sugar: 1.8g Protein: 2.6g | Sodium: 365mg

Curried Broccoli

Prep Time: 10 minutes | Cook Time: 15 minutes | Serve: 1

Ingredients:

- Olive oil, 1/2 tablespoon
- thinly sliced 1/4 of a small yellow onion 1/4 teaspoon chopped fresh ginger
- 1/2 tsp. curry powder
- 1/4 teaspoon of cumin seeds
- Add salt as needed.
- tbsp. of water
- 14 lb. of broccoli florets

Direction:

1. The onion should be sautéed in the oil for about 3–4 minutes over medium heat in a small nonstick skillet. Spices should be added now and sautéed for one to two minutes. Stir in the broccoli after adding the water.
2. Cook for around 3–4 minutes with the lid on at medium-high heat.
3. Serve warm.

Calories: 112 | Fat: 7.7g | Carbohydrates: 9.3g | Fiber: 3.8g | Sugar: 2.7g Protein: 3.6g | Sodium: 195mg

Broccoli With Bell Peppers

Prep Time: 10 minutes | Cook Time: 10 minutes | Serve: 1

Ingredients:

- 1/9 cup olive oil
- 1 chopped tiny garlic clove 1/4 sliced yellow onion
- 1 thinly sliced, seeded tiny bell pepper
- tiny broccoli florets, 14 cup
- 1/2 tsp. low-sodium soy sauce
- 2-3 teaspoons of vegetable broth low in sodium
- black pepper, ground as needed

Direction:

1. Melt the coconut oil in a nonstick wok over medium heat, then sauté the garlic for approximately a minute. Stir-fry the vegetables for about 5 minutes after adding them.
2. Add the stock and soy sauce, mix, and cook the vegetables for 4 minutes, or until they are cooked to your liking. Remove from the heat after adding the black pepper.
3. Serve warm.

Calories: 78 | Fat: 7.5g | Carbohydrates: 8.2g | Fiber: 25g | Sugar: 3.3g Protein: 2.3g | Sodium: 265mg

Cauliflower With Peas

Prep Time: 10 minutes | Cook Time: 15 minutes | Serve: 1

Ingredients:
- 1 sliced small tomato 1/4 cup olive oil, 2 teaspoons water
- 1 tiny clove of minced garlic
- 12 teaspoon minced fresh ginger
- 14 teaspoon of cumin, ground
- 1/4 teaspoon of coriander, ground
- a quarter teaspoon of cayenne
- a pinch of turmeric powder
- 1/4 cup chopped cauliflower
- 3 tablespoons freshly shelled green peas
- if needed, salt and freshly ground black pepper
- 3 to 4 tablespoons of hot water

Direction:
1. Tomato and 2 tablespoons of water should be added to a mini-blender and pulsed until a smooth puree forms. Place aside.
2. Heat the oil over medium heat in a small nonstick skillet, then sauté the garlic, ginger, and spices for approximately a minute. Cook the tomato puree, cauliflower, and peas while stirring for for 3–4 minutes. Bring to a boil after adding the heated water.
3. Cook covered for about 8 to 10 minutes, or until the vegetables are fully cooked, on medium-low heat.
4. Serve warm.

Calories: 139 | Fat: 11g | Carbohydrates: 9.4g | Fiber: 3.1g | Sugar: 3.9g Protein: 2.9g | Sodium: 165mg

Braised Cabbage

Prep Time: 10 minutes | Cook Time: 30 minutes | Serve: 1

Ingredients:

- 1/3 cup extra virgin olive oil
- a quarter of a tiny onion, finely sliced, and three-quarters of a cup of green cabbage
- water, 1/4 cup
- 1/2 tsp. erythritol
- Organic apple cider vinegar, 1/4 cup
- 1/4 tsp. caraway seeds
- Add salt as needed.

Direction:

1. The oil should be heated to medium heat before the cabbage, garlic, and onion are sautéed for around five minutes. Stir in the remaining ingredients after adding them.
2. As soon as possible, reduce the heat to low and simmer for 20 to 25 minutes.
3. Serve warm.

Calories: 63 | Fat: 4.8g | Carbohydrates: 5g | Fiber: 1.9g | Sugar: 2.4g Protein: 1g | Sodium: 165mg

Snacks and Appetizers Recipes

Cinnamon Apple Chips

Prep Time: 5 Minutes Cooking Time: 2 To 3 Hours Serving: 4

Ingredients:

- 4 apples
- 1 teaspoon ground cinnamon

Direction:

1. Set the oven to 200 °F. Use parchment paper to cover a baking sheet.
2. Apples should be cored and sliced into 1/8-inch rounds.
3. Mix the cinnamon and apple slices in a medium basin. On the prepared baking sheet, arrange the apples in a single layer.
4. Cook the apples for 2 to 3 hours, or until they are dry. While heated, they will still be mushy, but once totally cooled, they will become crisp. Store for up to four days in an airtight container.
Cooking tip: If you don't have parchment paper, use cooking spray to prevent sticking.

Nutrition: Calories: 96; Total Fat: 0g; Saturated Fat: 0g; Cholesterol: 0mg; Carbohydrates: 26g; Fiber: 5g; Protein: 1g; Phosphorus: 0mg; Potassium: 198mg; Sodium: 2mg

Homemade Rice Cakes

Prep time: 5 min, cooking time: 40-50 min, Servings: 12

Ingredients:

- 2 eggs and 210g of rice in 360ml of water
- two tablespoons of regular or gluten-free flour
- Your preferred flavors

For savory:

- 1 tsp salt
- 2 teaspoons Parmesan cheese
- pepper to taste

For cute:

- 2-3 envelopes of Trivia sweetener
- 1 tsp cinnamon

Direction:

1. the oven to 170 °C.
2. The uncooked rice should be processed or blended until it is powdery.
3. The remaining ingredients should be blended in a powerful food processor or blender.
4. In a muffin pan or greased domed pan, pour the batter.
5. Bake for 40 to 50 minutes, or until the top is golden and the edges are crispy..

Nutrition: Protein: 2 g , Fat: 4 g, Net Carbohydrates: 13 g

Easy and quick cheese dip

Prep time: 5 min cooking time: 0 min Servings: 12

Ingredients:

- cottage cheese, 240g
- three onions, spring
- 120 grams of sour cream
- Tabasco sauce, hot, 2 tablespoons
- 12 teaspoon garlic powder
- 1 teaspoon dill
- 75 g blue cheese crumbles

Direction:

1. Sour cream, cottage cheese, tabasco sauce, scallions, and spices should be blended to a creamy consistency in a food processor.
2. Add blue cheese and blend for a short while.
3. If desired, garnish with thinly sliced spring onions.

Nutrition: Protein: 4 g, Fat: 5 g, Net Carbohydrates: 3 g

Southwest Pozole

Prep time: 5 min, cooking time: 50 min, Servings: 6

Ingredients:

- 1 tablespoon of olive oil
- onion, 25g
- Pork fillet, 450 grams
- a single garlic clove
- 115 g sliced green chilies from a can
- White cornmeal, 790 g
- 940.00 ml of chicken broth (low sodium)
- Add a little black pepper

Directions:

1. Make 1-inch-long slices of pork. Chop the onion and garlic. It is necessary to drain and rinse cornmeal.
2. Sauté the pork chunks for three to four minutes in a skillet with heated oil over medium-high heat.
3. Add the onion and garlic to the pan. Fry the onion until it is tender.
4. The meat should be tender and the flavors should have melded after 30 to 45 minutes of simmering. Add some water if you need more liquid to prepare soup.
5. If desired, garnish with tortilla strips, shredded cabbage, radishes, cilantro, or lime juice.

Nutrition: Protein: 26 g, Fat: 13 g, Net Carbohydrates: 15 g

Donut

Prep time: 5 min cooking time: 10 min
Servings: 10

Ingredients:

- All-purpose flour, 85 grams
- 4 eggs
- 1 cup sugar
- skim milk, 240 ml
- Just a little vanilla extract

Direction:

1. The sugar and flour should be blended together in a medium mixing basin. Whisk the eggs well using a whisk.
2. In a mixing basin, combine milk and vanilla extract. Blend until the mixture is flawless.
3. 3 tablespoons of batter should be added to an 8x10 nonstick pan with cooking spray. Tilt the pan quickly to spread the batter. Bake the doughnut until the bottom is golden brown (about 45 seconds; the edges would start to dry). Cook the pancake's reverse side. In order to finish the batter, continue doing this.
4. Serve thin donuts folded or rolled with syrup, jam, or fruit spread. If preferred, fill with 1-2 teaspoons of cream cheese or ricotta.

Nutrition: Protein eats : 4 g, Fat: 2 g, Net Carbohydrates: 10 g

Garlic mashed potatoes

Prep time: 5 min cooking time: 15 min
Servings: 4

Ingredients:

- potatoes two
- 60g of butter
- 2 garlic cloves
- Low-fat milk in 60 ml

Direction:

1. Peeling and chopping potatoes into small pieces is recommended. Cook twice to reduce potassium levels if you're following a low-potassium diet.
2. Potatoes and garlic are cooked until they are soft over medium heat.
3. The pot's water should be drained.
4. Blend the garlic and potato garlic till creamy, then drizzle in the milk and butter gently.

Nutrition: Protein: 2 g, Fat: 13 g, Net Carbohydrates: 15 g

Turkey Sloppy Joe Burger

Prep time: 5 min cooking time: 15 min
Servings: 6

Ingredients:

- Red onions, 25 grams
- Ground turkey, 675 g
- Green peppers, 75 g
- 2 tbsp. brown sugar
- 1 tablespoon Mrs. Dash Grill Seasoning mixed with chicken
- Worcestershire sauce, 1 tablespoon
- hamburger buns, six
- Tomato sauce 225 grams (low sodium)

Direction:

1. Cut the onion and peppers into tiny pieces.
2. When the turkey is cooked, place it in a large pan and sear it over medium-high heat.
3. Combine Worcestershire sauce, Mrs. Dash seasoning, sugar, and tomato sauce in a small bowl. Spices are used to season the turkey combination. Cook for approximately 10 minutes on low heat.
4. Serve with hamburger buns, then cut into six pieces.

Nutrition: Protein: 24 g , Fat: 9 g, Net Carbohydrates: 28 g

Pineapple sauce

Prep time: 5 min cooking time: 0 min
Servings: 16

Ingredients:

- Treat of 280g canned pineapple juice
- a single garlic clove
- a 15 g onion
- 2 tbsp coriander
- 1 tablespoon jalapeo chili

Direction:

1. Chop the jalapenos, onions, garlic, and cilantro finely.
2. Place the pineapple in a bowl after draining.
3. Well combine the remaining ingredients.
4. Refrigerate for many hours, preferably overnight, to let the flavors to blend..

Nutrition: Protein: 0 g, Fat: 0 g, Net Carbohydrates: 4 g

Maryland Crab Cakes

Prep time: 5 min cooking time: 10 min
Servings: 6

Ingredients:

- 450 g of crab meat, lump
- 1 tablespoon mayo
- 1 white bread piece
- Old Bay seasoning, 1 teaspoon
- Yellow mustard, 1 teaspoon
- 1 egg
- 1-tablespoon fresh parsley
- One cayenne peppercorn
- 2/TBS of olive oil

Direction:

1. In a medium bowl, place the crab meat; remove any shell pieces.
2. Every bread piece should be cut into cubes. Chop the parsley to get it ready.
3. Mix the crab with the cayenne pepper, mayonnaise, toast, mustard, parsley, spices, Old Bay seasoning, and Old Bay seasoning mix. Gently incorporate all ingredients in the mixture.
4. Make six 2 cm-thick crab cakes. Place in the fridge for at least an hour.
5. Melt skillet's olive oil (ideally a cast iron skillet).
6. Crab cakes should bake for five minutes on each side or until golden. Serve right away.

Nutrition: Protein: 15 g , Fat: 8 g, Net Carbohydrates: 3 g

Cheese Tart

Prep time: 5 min cooking time: 10 min
Servings: 14

Ingredients:

- Cream cheese, 225g
- sugar, 150 grams
    - 2 eggs
    - 1 teaspoon vanilla extract
    - 12 vanilla waffles in total
    - 12 paper muffin liners
- Apple pie filling, 105 grams

Direction:

1. Before creating tartlets, give cream cheese an hour to soften.
2. the oven to 170 °C.
3. The sugar, eggs, cream cheese, and vanilla extract should be thoroughly combined in a mixing dish.
4. Place muffin cups in a muffin pan. A vanilla waffle should be put into each mold.
5. Fill vanilla waffle with cream cheese mixture to the 3/4 mark.
6. For ten minutes, bake. The tarts should be taken out of the oven and put in the refrigerator to cool.
7. Place 1 tablespoon and a half of pie filling on top of each tart right before serving.

Nutrition: Protein: 2 g, Fat: 8 g, Net Carbohydrates: 28 g

Lemon Pepper Hummus

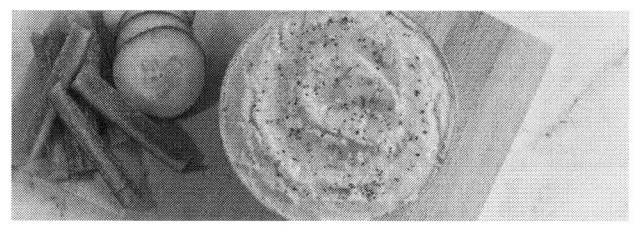

Prep time: 5 min cooking time: 0 min Servings: 10

Ingredients:

- canned chickpeas, 850 g
- 80 ml from 1 lemon. Almond oil
  - 1 tsp of the seasoning lemon pepper (salt free)
- Just a little garlic powder

Direction:

1. The chickpeas should be added to a blender or food processor after draining and washing.
2. Leave 1 tablespoon of olive oil aside. Combine the leftover lemon pepper spice, olive oil, garlic powder, and lemon juice with the chickpeas.
3. Blend or process until uniform. If required, dilute with 2 to 3 teaspoons of water.
4. Add the item to a mixing bowl and top with the final tablespoon of olive oil..

Nutrition: Protein: 3 g , Fat: 8 g, Net Carbohydrates: 11 g

Sandwich with potatoes and egg

Prep time: 5 min cooking time: 15 min Servings: 4

Ingredients:

- 1 potato –6 eggs
- 2 tbsp canola oil–4 tsp. salsa
- 4 wheat sandwiches

Direction:

1. Potato dice are placed in a pan that has been heated with oil. Cook the potatoes now until they are golden brown.
2. After beating the eggs, pour them over the potatoes. Once eggs are set, turn heat down to low and continue mixing potatoes for an additional 2-3 minutes.
3. Among the thin sandwiches, distribute the potato and egg mixture equally. If desired, top each sandwich with a teaspoon of salsa. Offer and savor.

Nutrition: Protein: 16 g , Fat: 15 g, Net Carbohydrates: 32 g

Low-Fat Mango Salsa

Prep Time: 10 minutes Cooking Time: 10 minutes Servings: 4

Ingredients:

- 1 cup chopped cucumber, 2 cups diced mango, and 1/2 cup minced cilantro
- 2 teaspoons of lime juice, fresh
- 1 tablespoon minced scallions
- 1/4 tsp. chipotle powder
- 1/4 tsp. sea salt

Direction

The ingredients should be combined in a bowl before serving or chilling.

Nutrition: Calories: 155 Fat: 0.6 g Carbs: 38.2 g Protein: 1.4 g Sodium: 3.2 mg Potassium: 221mg Phosphorus: 27mg

Easy No-Bake Coconut Cookies

Prep Time: 5 minutes Cooking Time: 10 minutes Servings: 20

Ingredients:

- 3 cups of flakes of finely crushed coconut
- 1 cup of coconut oil, melted
- 1 teaspoon stevia liquid

Direction:

1. In a big bowl, combine all the ingredients and whisk until well combined.
2. Place the mixture's little balls on a baking sheet covered with paper.
3. Refrigerate until solid, then press a fork into the bottom of each biscuit. Enjoy!

Nutrition: Calories: 99 Fat: 10 g Carbs: 2 g Protein: 3 Sodium: 7 m Potassium: 105mg Phosphorus: 11mg

Index

Break-Fast Recipes 12
- Holy Eggs 13
- Lemon Blueberry Surprise Muffins 13
- New Baked Garlic 14
- Broccoli Dip in French Bread 14
- Deviled Eggs 15
- New Mexican Nibbles 15
- Instant Pot Nuts & Bolts 16
- Nectarine Bruschetta 16
- Egg Muffins With Ham .. 17
- Kale Frittata with Sweet Potato 17
- Avocado, Black Bean, and Quinoa Salad 18
- Garlic-Mint Scrambled Eggs 18
- Healthy Fruit Smoothie 19
- Zucchini with Egg 19
- Green Slime Smoothie ... 20
- Goat Cheese and Spinach Egg Muffs 20
- Fruit and Cheese Breakfast Wrap 21
- Mozzarella Cheese Omelet 21
- Herb Frittata 22
- Spinach-Curry Crepes ... 22

Beef Recipes 23
- Beef With Mushrooms .. 24
- Beef With Bell Peppers . 24
- Basil Ground Beef 25
- Ground Beef With Cabbage 25
- Beef Avocado Cup 26
- Lemony Pork Chop 26
- Rosemary Lamb Chop ... 27
- Lamb Koftas 27
- Spiced Beef Meatballs ... 28
- Beef Avocado Cup 28
- Roast Beef 29
- Spiced Lamb Burgers 29
- Pork Loins with Leeks ... 30
- Bacon-Wrapped Mozzarella Sticks 30

Poultry Recipes 31
- Crispy chicken wraps 32
- Italian Chicken Salad 32
- Apple Chicken Crispy Salad 33
- Chicken Scampi 33
- Chicken and Apple Curry 34
- Turkey & Veggie Salad .. 34
- Turkey Lettuce Wraps .. 35
- Seasoned Turkey Legs .. 35
- Turkey With Mushrooms 36
- Ground Turkey In Tomato Sauce 36
- Ground Turkey with Pumpkin 37
- Duck Breast 37
- Spiced Quail 38
- Lemony Chicken Drumstick 38

Fish Recipes 39
- Baked Fish in Cream Sauce 40
- Shrimp & Broccoli 40
- Shrimp in Garlic Sauce .. 41
- Baked Trout 41
- Broiled Shrimp 42
- Grilled Lemony Cod 42
- Cucumber Bites, Smoked Salmon And Avocado 43
- Broiled Salmon Fillets ... 43
- Herbed Vegetable Trout 44
- Lemon Pepper Trout 44
- Fish With Mushrooms ... 45
- Parsley Scallops 45
- Shrimp with Zucchini Noodles 46
- Grilled Tilapia Tacos 46
- Tuna & Egg Salad 47
- Shrimp & Olives Salad ... 47
- Shrimp & Avocado Salad 48
- Shrimp & Corn Salad 48
- Scallops & Tomato Salad 49
- Shrimp Lettuce Wraps .. 49

Soup Recipes 50
- Cauliflower & Pear Soup 51
- Chicken & Rice Soup 51

Corn and fennel soup 52
Thai fish soup 52
Spring Pea Soup 53
Canadian stew 53
Shiitake broth 54
Turkey Burger Soup 54
Barbeque Sauce 55
Basic Dressing 55
Lemon ice cream torte .. 57
Bagel bread pudding 57
Mint Melted Chocolate Brownies 58
Saskatoon Berry Pudding 58
Strawberries with balsamic vinegar and basil 59
Almond Meringue Cookies 59
Apple Blueberry Crumb Cake 60
Raspberry Crumble Muffins 60
Vanilla Custard 61
Bread Pudding 61
Strawberry Ice Cream ... 62
Baked Peaches with Cream Cheese 62
Gingerbread-muffins 63
Zucchini Brownies 63
Strawberries with balsamic vinegar and basil 64

Raspberry Cheesecake Mousse 64

Salad Recipes 65

Chicken and Mandarin Salad 66
Tuna macaroni salad 66
Fruity zucchini salad 67
Hawaiian Chicken Salad 67
Macaroni Salad 68
Grapes Jicama Salad 68
Italian Cucumber Salad . 69
Barb's Asian Slaw 69
Green Bean and Potato Salad 70
Pear & Brie Salad 70
Caesar Salad 71
Thai Cucumber Salad 71
Cream Cheese Herb Toasts 73
Aubergine puree 73
Vegan Pie (White Bean Spread) 74
Simple Roasted Broccoli 74
Roasted Mint Carrots 75
Roasted Asparagus 75
Vinegar & Salt Kale 76
Lemony Brussels Sprout 76
Simple Asparagus 77
Gingered Asparagus 77
Balsamic Asparagus 78

Spiced Mushrooms 78
Parsley Mushrooms 79
Mushroom With Spinach 79
Herbed Cauliflower 80
Garlicky Broccoli 80
Curried Broccoli 81
Broccoli With Bell Peppers 81
Cauliflower With Peas ... 82
Braised Cabbage 82

Snacks and Appetizers Recipes 83

Cinnamon Apple Chips .. 84
Homemade Rice Cakes .. 84
Easy and quick cheese dip 85
Southwest Pozole 85
Donut 86
Garlic mashed potatoes 86
Turkey Sloppy Joe Burger 87
Pineapple sauce 87
Maryland Crab Cakes 88
Cheese Tart 88
Lemon Pepper Hummus 89
Sandwich with potatoes and egg 89
Low-Fat Mango Salsa 90
Easy No-Bake Coconut Cookies 90

Final Words

If you've been waiting for the final chapter of my RENAL DIET COOKBOOK, hold your horses because we've here! In this last section, I'll review a few general aspects of the diet and provide my own opinions.

First, one of the most important aspects of calculating your net fluid balance is understanding how much fluid you consume daily. Otherwise, you won't be able to tell how out of the compensation you are. I know that many of you are following this diet without a weighing scale, so I'll give you some pointers on how to do it correctly.

First, you should obtain a testing instrument. There are numerous decent ones on the market now that can tell you how much fluid is entering and exiting the system (e.g., blood test, urine test, etc.)

Following the diet is critical to maintaining an exact journal of everything you eat and how much liquids you consume. If you forget about it for the day or have unexpected visitors, I recommend going back and changing your daily balance accordingly. Many individuals would say, "oh well," because they periodically consume more food or drink more fluid (water, juice, etc.), leading to bad long-term results. If this occurs, go back through your logbook and recalculate.

Also, salt levels can significantly alter your estimate of net fluid balance. I strongly advise you to monitor the salt amount of everything you consume. For example, if you eat a salty item or even just a few sips of juice, add that extra sodium to your daily total. Similarly, if you are eating or drinking something with very low salt (e.g., rice sausages), remove a few tablespoons per day to ensure accurate results.

The third concern I'd want to bring out is that some people have experienced dehydration while on this diet. If you realize that you have been drinking too much fluid (i.e., peeing too frequently) or have a chronic dry mouth, you may be dehydrated. Don't be concerned. Drinking enough water while on this diet, preferably at least 8 ounces every hour, is crucial. However, some people cannot handle the extra fluid and will become dehydrated. If this happens to you, reduce your fluid intake and try again in a few days (if you must).

Finally, I believe that an overabundance of protein causes the bulk of dehydration instances in persons on this diet. Most people are accustomed to consuming enough protein to fulfill their body's requirements daily. When you replace all of it with homemade food, you'll quickly run out of protein. As a result, I highly advise that protein intake be limited to roughly 1 gram per pound of body weight every day (e.g.,

150 grams if you weigh 150 pounds). Even if you've been eating more than this, try cutting back and seeing how you feel.

Made in the USA
Columbia, SC
29 August 2023